MORE HESSELBEIN ON LEADERSHIP

MORE HESSELBEIN ON LEADERSHIP

FRANCES HESSELBEIN

FOREWORD BY JAMES M. KOUZES

JOSSEY-BASS
A Wiley Imprint
www.josseybass.com

Published by Jossey-Bass
A Wiley Imprint
One Montgomery Street, Suite 1200, San Francisco, CA 94104-4594.

Jossey-Bass books and products are available through most bookstores. To contact Jossey-Bass directly call our Customer Care Department within the U.S. at 800-956-7739, outside the U.S. at 317-572-3986, or fax 317-572-4002.

Jossey-Bass also publishes its books in a variety of electronic formats. Some content that appears in print may not be available in electronic books.

Library of Congress Cataloging-in-Publication Data available upon request:

Printed in the United States of America
FIRST EDITION
PB Printing 10 9 8 7 6 5 4 3 2 1

CONTENTS

FOREWORD

A Call to Serve

To lead is to serve.

This is the theme that defines Frances Hesselbein's life. And it's the dominant theme of this book.

There is no one better qualified to teach us about servant leadership than Frances. From her very early days as a Girl Scouts executive director in Johnstown, Pennsylvania, to her more recent two-year appointment as the Class of '51 Chair for the Study of Leadership at West Point, Frances exemplifies what it means to answer the call to serve. And it's a call that all of us must answer if we're going to be authentic leaders.

Alan Mulally, whom Frances mentions in the very first essay, would agree. Alan is the president and CEO of the Ford Motor Company and was the first person to be awarded the Leader of the Future by the Frances Hesselbein Leadership Institute (formerly the Leader to Leader Institute and the Peter F. Drucker Foundation for Nonprofit Management). In an interview with the *Washington Post*, Alan was asked, "How has your leadership style changed over the years? What have you learned? What do you know now that you didn't use to?" Alan responded:

> I think that just always remembering that we're here to serve. We have the honor to be selected to be the leader, but we're actually serving our customers, we're serving our employees, and the more that you have a servant perspective or a servant attitude, then the more inclusion you'll have, the more respect for people's ideas [you'll have].[1]

Alan maintained that this servant attitude played a large part in the turnaround process at Ford during the difficult years at the end of the twenty-first century's opening decade. It's no wonder that Alan has such high regard for Frances's leadership philosophy and practice. He knows, as do countless other friends and colleagues of Frances Hesselbein, that she is absolutely correct: To lead is to serve.

As I read through the essays in this book, I found that a certain calm came over me. It was as if I were meditating. I think you'll experience the same thing. There's a graciousness to Frances's writing, just as there's graciousness to the person. She writes with an elevating tone. She invites us to lead with our best selves.

As I reflected on her writing, a few key messages emerged for me about what it means to lead and serve. Those messages are:

- Leadership is local.
- Leadership is from the inside out.
- Leaders engage others.
- Leaders initiate change.
- Leaders go first.
- Leaders sustain hope.

Here are my reflections on these lessons.

Leadership Is Local

In the opening essay, "A Long and Exuberant Journey," Frances says that "leadership is not a title." Amen to that. If there is one thing I can say for certain after researching leadership for over 30 years with my colleague and coauthor Barry Posner, it is that leadership is not about position or title. It's not about organizational power or authority. It's not about celebrity or wealth. It's not about the family you are born into. It's not about being a CEO, president, general, or prime minister. It's not about any of these things. It's about your relationship with others, your personal credibility, and about what you *do*.

You don't have to look up for leadership. You don't have to look out for leadership. You only have to look inward. You have the potential to lead others to places they have never been before. The true heroes of leadership are the ordinary people who get extraordinary things done. They are the men and women from all over the globe, from all walks of life and ages, and from a variety of organizations who struggle daily to lead us to greatness. They're the people who might live next door or work in the next cubicle over.

It's not surprising then to learn in "The Defining Moment" that the most influential person in Frances's early life was her grandmother. That revelation is consistent with what we find in our research. Family members are the number-one source of leader-role models—nearly twice as important as any other source. Teachers and coaches are second for young people and third for working adults, so it's also no wonder that Frances acknowledges throughout this book the profound influence Peter Drucker had on her, on the Girl Scouts of the USA, and on the Leader to Leader Institute. Grandmothers and teachers don't often appear as case studies in most MBA or leadership development programs, but they ought to.

The data are very clear on this. The most important leaders are those who are closest to us. If you're a manager in an organization, to your direct reports you are more likely than any other leader to influence their desire to stay or leave, the trajectory of their careers, their ethical behavior, their ability to perform at their best, their drive to wow customers, their satisfaction with their jobs, and their motivation to share the organization's vision and values. If you're a parent, teacher, coach, or community leader, you are the person who's setting the leadership example for young people. You are the one they are most likely going to look to for the example of how a leader responds to competitive situations, handles crises, deals with loss, or resolves ethical dilemmas. It's not someone else. It's you.

Leadership is a choice—*your* choice. The quality of leadership those closest to you get is entirely up to you. And when you choose to lead every day, you enlist in a very special relationship with others. It's one you should cherish, because you have the awesome opportunity—and responsibility—to make a profound difference in the lives of others.

Leadership Is From the Inside Out

Authentic leadership does not come from the outside in. It comes from the inside out. Inside-out leadership means becoming the author of your own story and the maker of your own history. All serious leadership starts from within.

In three of her essays—"A Long and Exuberant Journey," "Seeing Things Whole," and "Emerging Leaders"—Frances speaks to the issue of values. She tells us that all leaders will have to answer questions such as "Who is that leader within? If I am expressing myself in my work, what are my ethics, my beliefs, my values, my philosophy?"

People always want to know something about the person doing the leading before they're going to become the people doing the following. They want to know about who you are, where you come from, what you care about, and why they ought to be following you. They want to know what gives you the confidence to think that you can actually pull this off.

In "Emerging Leaders," Frances tells us that the young and upcoming leaders express "enormous interest in values, how you live them, and what to do if you are expected to violate your own principles in the workplace." Emerging leaders are much more willing to acknowledge that they are values-focused and mission-driven than prior generations. Our data suggest that today at least 65 percent of leaders want to talk openly about values at work. Values are no longer taboo topics to be avoided or discussed in hushed tones. They are top of mind, and front and center. Emerging leaders are sending a very powerful message about the importance of trust, ethics, and integrity, and it's time to pay attention.

But inside-out leading doesn't mean that you simply impose your values on others. You also have to appreciate, Frances says, ". . . the customer who is listened to, partners whose collaboration is essential in our work, and a vision of the future that shimmers in the distance. . . . Pulling out one piece, one action, one aspect of the leadership challenge is like playing a one-string guitar—noise but not much music." To make harmonious music, leaders have to play all the strings. Personal values are the starting place, but you also must build commitment to shared values and a shared vision, and you must get people to see themselves as part of a larger whole—as part of a community in which survival and success depend on a common understanding of purpose and principles.

Leaders Engage Others

Leadership is a relationship. It's a relationship between those you aspire to lead and those who choose to follow. To remain strong, relationships have to be nurtured. You have to stay in touch, and you have to stay in touch often. You have to do it with family and friends, and you have to do it with constituents.

In "The Key to Cultural Transformation," Frances writes, "Changes in the practices and beliefs of an organization do not happen because someone sits in the executive office and commands them." Instead, you earn them through engagement. You earn them through human contact—in the hallways, on patient floors, in classrooms, in cubicles, on factory floors, in retail shops, and on the streets. You earn them when you shake a hand, ask a question, and listen to what others have to say.

Frances also writes in "The Art of Listening" that leading means listening. Listening, she says, is a sign of respect, appreciation, and anticipation. When it comes to leading, talking is highly overrated. Listening is far more important to effective leadership.

Listening is a two-way street, of course. That means, as Frances discusses in "The Indispensable Partnership," that boards and CEOs need to appreciate each other and the important and distinctive roles they play. Leadership is a team effort. You can't do it alone. Boards, management, funders, and staff have to collaborate. Frances asks us to focus on what we can do together to solve today's problems and create tomorrow's future.

"I've known for a long time that my work—my style of leadership and management—is inclusive and circular," Frances tells us. One of the most important lessons I learned from Frances was from a question she told me she asked when she first assumed the role as CEO of the Girl Scouts of the USA. She asked board and staff to answer this: "When they look at us, can they find themselves?" Just think what it means to be able to see yourself in the vision, values, products, services, and culture of an organization.

In a very moving story telling of her encounter with an Army soldier in an airport, Frances talks about the "faces in the crowd." She says, "Whenever I see one of our soldiers in uniform in an airport, I always go up and say, 'I hope you understand how much we appreciate what you are doing for all of us and our country.'" In this short piece, she shows the power of engagement, the power of reaching out to other human beings and connecting with them at their core. This story also illustrates how engagement requires never being so busy with your own agenda that you have no time to talk with anyone who isn't already on the schedule—or that your schedule is so full that people have to wait forever to get an appointment and lose interest in the issue, and in you. As busy as she is, she always has time for others.

In "Together, We Can Change the World," Frances reminds us that it will take all of us to build healthy communities. Her little acts of kindness contribute to doing just that. Frances goes further in "The Leaders We Need," saying, "The leader as a healer and a unifier ought to be high on our leadership checklist." What could we accomplish together if all leaders adopted the perspective that they were healers and unifiers? The possibilities are astounding when you think about it.

Leaders Initiate Change

Leaders are no strangers to challenges. All you have to do is reflect on leaders throughout history. Barry Posner and I have been asking people for three decades to think about historical leaders they admire—leaders they'd willingly follow if the leaders were alive today. The lesson from this simple exercise is always the same: Challenge is central to every situation.

When people talk about social sector, government, or military leaders, for example, they discuss men and women who liberated people from tyranny, fought for human rights, won wars, struggled against oppression, organized movements for change, or suffered greatly for their causes. When people think of the business leaders they admire, they think about people who have turned around failing companies, started entrepreneurial ventures, developed breakthrough products and services, or transformed industries. Challenge was the context in which these leaders operated, and change was the theme of all their campaigns.

You don't have to study historical leaders to learn this lesson. You can just look at everyday leaders such as yourself and those down the hall or across the street. When we first analyzed the initial set of personal best leadership cases nearly three decades ago, what immediately struck us was that people always chose situations in which they were challenged in very significant ways.

Leadership and change are simply inseparable. Sometimes leaders have to initiate the change and shake things up. Other times they just have to grab hold of the adversity that surrounds them. Whether challenge comes from the outside or the inside, leaders make things happen. Frances calls these folks "rock climbers" in "The Winter of Our Concern," and she reminds us that they are "taking the lead to build a better future." She also reminds us, in "Crisis Management: A Leadership Imperative," that we have to prepare ourselves for the challenges ahead. She says, "Crisis management is not a discipline to be learned on the job, in the midst of the storm. It must be learned and practiced when there's not a cloud in the organizational sky."

To be a leader, you need to make something happen. You need to take charge of change. You need to feel a strong sense of commitment, believing that you can find something in whatever you are doing that is interesting, important, or worthwhile.

Leaders Go First

Changing hearts, minds, and lives requires a deep level of commitment. Authentic leaders are the first to demonstrate that kind of commitment. They are the first to put the guiding principles of the organization ahead of all else. They are the first to do what has been agreed upon. They are the first to demonstrate that they are not in it for themselves, but instead have the best interests of the institution, department, or team and its constituents at heart. They are the first to hold themselves accountable for their actions.

There are lots of common phrases for this kind of leadership. *Walk the talk, practice what you preach, put your money where your mouth is,* and *follow through on your promises* are some of them. They all mean the same thing. Your actions had better be consistent with your words. The truth is that you either lead by example or you don't lead at all.

Quite often the greatest distance that leaders have to travel is the distance from their mouths to their feet. Taking that step toward fulfilling a promise, putting the resources behind a pledge, and acting on a verbal commitment may require great courage. But it's the very thing that demonstrates the courage of your convictions.

Leaders should also be the first to sacrifice and the first to suffer. In "In Service to the Common Good," Frances says quite boldly that, if she were in charge, she "would institute national and community service for every 18-year-old man and woman in the United States. They would serve 18 months or two years." It could be any kind of service, but she'd make sure that everyone had the privilege of serving the country in some way. As an old Peace Corps volunteer, I have to say that this warmed my heart. I was uplifted by the dream she describes when she writes, "Shimmering far in the distance is our vision of the future: a country with citizens who care about all of our people, and young men and women called, eager to serve leaders at every level sustaining the democracy."

In this age of reality shows like *Survivor, The Apprentice,* and *The Amazing Race,* it sometimes appears that these are quaint notions long past their prime. But not to Frances Hesselbein. Nor to any of the successful leaders she discusses in this book. To them, it is an honor to serve. It's an honor to go first. Their measure of success is whether those who are served grow—whether they become healthier, wiser, freer, more autonomous, more capable—and whether they become leaders in their own right.

Leaders Sustain Hope

Frances reminds us in "Beyond the Distracting Clamor, We Hear the Leaders of the Future" and "An Antidote to Cynicism" that our country, and the world, are experiencing the lowest levels of trust and the highest levels of cynicism in decades. Frances laments but she doesn't despair. And she exhorts us not to despair either.

Frances isn't at all intimidated by the challenging realities we now face. In fact, she says she's full of hope. She is full of hope because of the new generation of leaders now taking the stage, and she is full of hope because of her faith in the human race.

Hope is essential to achieving the highest levels of performance. Hope is also vital to an active and healthy life. All leaders must keep hope alive. They have to strengthen people's belief that the struggle they are called upon to deal with will produce a more promising future. Frances is absolutely right. The only antidote to the increased cynicism and stresses of these times is renewed faith in human capacity and an intensely optimistic belief that together leaders and constituents can overcome the difficulties of today and tomorrow.

Hope enables us to transcend the difficulties, to bounce back after being stressed, stretched, and depressed, to find the will and the way to aspire to greatness. Hope is testimony to the power of the human spirit.

Barry Posner and I have found in our research that people want leaders who are positive and optimistic. They want leaders who are inspiring and full of hope for the future. It's part of what makes a leader credible. It's part of what attracts people to leaders in the first place.

Frances's life and writings illuminate the positive power of positive leadership. In "The Inspiring Journey We All Share," Frances tells a wonderfully humorous story about what her husband John said she'd say if she were drowning. I won't spoil the punch line for you, but it's another example of vintage Frances: always finding the positive when it's ever so easy to give in to the negative.

People feed off of their leaders' moods and their leaders' views of the world. Positive leaders arouse optimistic feelings and enable their constituents to hold confident thoughts about success. Positivity stretches our minds, opens us up to new possibilities, and expands our worldviews. Positive leadership breeds positive emotions. In the final essay in this little gem of a book, Frances says, "Life is circular." What goes around comes around. That's the way it is with human emotions. If you want positive actions from positive people, the circle starts with you. Call it the physics of leadership: positives attract, negatives repel.

Frances Hesselbein never expected early in her life that she'd one day be the CEO of the largest organization supporting girls in this country. She never imagined that she'd earn an appointment to a chair at West Point. She never imagined that she'd become the CEO of the Peter F. Drucker Foundation for Nonprofit Management and that the organization would today be known as the Frances Hesselbein Leadership Institute. These things were never in her career plan. But opportunity knocked, and she was prepared to answer the door.

Just like Frances, none of us really knows when we might get another call to lead. It could come tonight. It could come tomorrow. It could come next year. It could come at anytime. You just never know. Are you ready to answer the call when it comes? Are you ready to lead from within, to engage others, to take initiative, to go first, and to sustain hope? Are you ready?

What we learn from Frances is that each of us could be called many times to make a meaningful difference and to have a positive impact on the lives of others. It's not a question of "Will I make a difference?" The question is "What difference will I make?" The essays in this book will help you find your own answer to that question. And you need to. Because you just never know.

—**Jim Kouzes**

1. On leadership: Ford CEO Alan Mulally on the 'liberating clarity' of his mission. (2012, March 3). *Washington Post On Leadership.* Retrieved from http://www.washingtonpost.com/wp-dyn/content/video/2010/03/17 /VI2010031700383.html.

INTRODUCTION

Rarely has there been a stronger call in our country for principled, ethical, effective leadership. And every day, my definition of leadership as "a matter of how to be, not how to do" becomes more cogent, more logical, and more imperative. This is the message that is the basis of everything I write about, speak about, and try to live: "Leadership is a matter of how to be, not how to do. It is the quality and character of the leader that determines the performance, the results."

This was the essence of my work with the Girl Scouts of the USA for 13 years and was the basis of our adventure in leadership with the Peter F. Drucker Foundation for Nonprofit Management, later named the Leader to Leader Institute, and, in January 2012, the Frances Hesselbein Leadership Institute. For 21 years, there was a common vision, a common mission, and the same definition of leadership.

Situations may change, demands may escalate, action plans may vary, and goals may even be revised to meet the new realities, yet the basic leadership values and principles never change. It is the quality and character of the leader that determines the performance, the results.

I hope that the words in the columns collected for this book, written across the years, will speak to you in ways that reflect and inspire your individual and organizational leadership journeys.

There are many rewarding aspects of writing my column for each issue of *Leader to Leader*. In particular, I love hearing (both in the letters I receive and in person) how our readers have applied what they've read to their own work. Or how something I've written has particularly touched their lives or provided the right amount of inspiration at just the right time. I'm continually reminded how connected all of us really are as we create and implement our visions of the future for ourselves and our organizations across all sectors.

But writing is not without its challenges. In each column, I want to make sure that I am doing justice to the ideas of the remarkable leaders and organizations I am describing. Have I adequately captured their capabilities and accomplishments? Have I fully described the opportunities open to leaders? These considerations are reflected by the daily challenges of being a leader in our rapidly changing world.

Each column allows me to take some time to examine my own experience in leadership, and the necessity for "seeing life whole." As I note in one of the columns within, "Seeing our lives whole is an even greater challenge than seeing our world of work whole."

My journey to leadership is a never-ending journey—learning every day of my life and finding fellow travelers who brighten the way. All of us are called to "shine a light."

Thank you for sharing the journey and permitting me to share it with you in *More Hesselbein on Leadership*. To serve is to live.

—Frances Hesselbein

PART I

The Personal Side of Leadership

A Long and Exuberant Journey

In my last year with the Girl Scouts of the USA, Warren Bennis published a book, *On Becoming a Leader*, in which he profiled 30 leaders after interviewing 100. The book was so successful that he made a videotape, "The Leader Within," with three leaders from the book: Max De Pree, chairman of Herman Miller, General Dave Palmer, superintendent of West Point, and me.

I wondered what office furniture, cadets at West Point, and a Brownie troop in South Central Los Angeles would have in common. We were filmed separately, and when the great day came when we received the finished videotape, it was amazing how—with three very different faces, very different lives—Warren found powerful commonalities, common lessons in leadership. I've always remembered one line toward the end of the video. He looks into the camera and says, "These three people never started out to become leaders. They began to express themselves in their work and, along the way, they became leaders." I often use his perception with young people on college campuses, the leaders of the future who are wondering how and when this moment will happen, the moment when they are recognized as leaders. They ask, "How will I know when I get there?" Somehow to them, "expressing yourself in your work" sounds reasonable, measurable. Warren's wisdom helps all of us to realize that becoming a leader is not a destination but a long and exuberant journey.

Increasingly, we recognize that leadership is not a title. Too often the chairmen, the presidents, the CEOs of enterprises in all three sectors have achieved the title, but leadership eludes them. Today, there are too many examples of failed leadership, failed initiatives, dispirited people within and outside the organization.

This column is too short to list the tragic examples of highly visible leaders who failed to give principled, ethical, mission-focused, values-based leadership. In the end they failed. The "leader within" was out to lunch.

When I am attempting to define leadership in ways that will connect, I often turn to Peter Drucker's wisdom, his genius in distilling the language into short, inspiring concepts that are powerful, relevant to our own times, our own situations. New books on leadership appear by the hundreds, most of them with something of value to add to any leadership philosophy. To these I add four insights that Peter Drucker distilled from his lifetime of introspection, observation, consultation. These are the four:

"The only definition of a leader is someone who has followers. Some people are thinkers. Some are prophets. Both roles are important and badly needed. But without followers, there can be no leaders."

"An effective leader is not someone who is loved or admired. He or she is someone whose followers do the right things. Popularity is not leadership. Results are."

"Leaders are highly visible. They therefore set examples."

"Leadership is not rank, privileges, titles, or money. It is responsibility."

Add to this Jim Collins's concept of the Level Five leader who "builds enduring greatness through a paradoxical blend of personal humility and professional will," and it is possible to appreciate how powerful was Warren Bennis's observation, "they expressed themselves in their work and they became leaders."

Of course, to young leaders of the future, or to leaders at any point along the way, the questions are, Who is that leader within? If I am expressing myself in my work, what are my ethics, my beliefs, my values, my philosophy? What do I believe, what do I value? Is my behavior consistent with my beliefs?

If observers say of us, "They expressed themselves in their work, and along the way they became leaders," then "know thyself" is a critical component.

Sometimes in speeches, or working with university students, I state the U.S. Army Warrior Ethos.

I will always place the mission first.
I will never accept defeat.
I will never quit.
I will never leave a fallen comrade.

And some of these MBA students translate the Warrior Ethos into their own language, their own situation, their own lives. It is not about the ethos of the U.S. Army. It is about them.

One inspiring example of a young leader who gives me hope for the future is Second Lieutenant Ben Tolle, graduate of West Point, Class of 2005, commanding a company of young soldiers in Baghdad. The e-mail messages I've received from him have no complaints, only praise for the remarkable young men and women in his command. Several months ago, e-mail arrived from Baghdad from Ben saying he was coming home and would be stationed near Nashville.

Dear Frances:
I am nearly out of Iraq and complete with my first deployment. Do you know of any nonprofit where I could volunteer a couple of afternoons or evenings a week in Nashville? Helping work events, fundraising, or planning?

Of course his e-mail and my message went immediately to several great nonprofit organizations in Nashville. And I just happened to be speaking in Nashville a short time later to 250 community leaders. Have you any doubt about what was the most inspiring part of my speech? Or that Lt. Ben's presence stays with me—a leader of the present, the leader of the future? He expresses himself in his work, knowing that leadership is a journey, not a destination.

Another example of a leader who gives me hope is Alan Mulally, the new president of Ford Motor Co. and the recipient of our first annual Leader of the Future Award.

Alan Mulally has never had a job. He always has been called to serve. His brilliant record is long and well documented—the record of a great leader with a passion for his calling. Always committed to the mission—the purpose of the enterprise. Always living the values, always the visionary—seeing the big picture of creating vehicles as a way to bring people together, in our country, in the world, connecting people to people, creating the better community, the better world. His transformation of Boeing Commercial Airplanes is legendary. Business school students study his exemplary case, his enormous success, created and sustained against fierce competition.

All his life Alan Mulally has kept before him a vision of the healthy community that cares about all of its people, expressing this in his work, believing that we are here "to love and be loved," as his mother taught him long ago.

When I called Alan several months ago to ask if we could honor him with our first Leader of the Future Award, his response was, "Oh, Frances, you don't mean me." That's Level Five leadership all the way. For Alan, leadership is not a title.

It happens at any age, at any time when we express ourselves in our work and along the way we become leaders. When this journal reaches you, we will have celebrated the winter holidays. I had eight family members around our Thanksgiving dinner table in Easton, Pennsylvania, and celebrated Christmas with my son and his family in Sacramento. All during the winter holidays, I tried to list my blessings, against the anxieties of our times. The blessings won, hands down. And high on the list were the readers and authors of *Leader to Leader*. Being surrounded by generous friends and contributors, the *Leader to Leader* family brightens the days, illuminates the journey, and shines a light as only you all can do. I am grateful.

This article originally appeared in *Leader to Leader*, Issue 44, Spring 2007.

The Defining Moment

I was speaking to a large group of chief learning officers, and after my speech, we had a very open and engaging dialogue. The last question asked was, "Mrs. Hesselbein, what was the one defining moment that determined the person you would be—the leader you would become?" No one had ever asked me this before, yet I knew the answer and immediately responded. Long ago, when I was eight years old, I was visiting my grandparents in South Fork, Pennsylvania, a small coal mining and railroad town. My grandfather had a men's clothing store, was justice of the peace, and played the pipe organ in the Methodist Church every Sunday.

I adored my grandparents and spent every weekend with Mama and Papa Wicks. They had seven children, so they needed a big house—and it seemed only logical to them to build into their house a pipe organ in a music room with a sixteen-foot ceiling. That room, with stained glass windows that caught the sunlight, was my favorite place. On the shelf above the pipe organ keyboard were two beautiful old Chinese vases. I would coax my grandmother to let me play with them and she always said no. Finally, on this Saturday visit, when I was eight years old, feeling very assertive, I stamped my foot at my grandmother and demanded that I be allowed to play with the vases. Instead of scolding me, my grandmother led me over to a small love seat facing the pipe organ, put her arms around me, and told me this story.

Long ago, when your mother was eight years old, some days she and her little sisters would come home from school crying that the bad boys were chasing Mr. Yee and calling him bad names. Now in this little town was a Chinese laundry man, who lived alone in his small laundry. Each week he picked up your grandfather's shirts and brought them back in a few days, washed, starched, ironed perfectly. Mr. Yee wore traditional Chinese dress—a long tunic, a cap with his hair in a queue. The boys would tease him, calling him, "Chinkey, Chinkey Chinaman," and other unkind names, and they would try to pull his queue.

One day there was a knock on the kitchen door. When I opened it, there stood Mr. Yee, with a large package in his arms. I said, "Oh, Mr. Yee, please come in. Won't you sit down?" But Mr. Yee just stood there and handed me the package, saying, "This is for you." I opened the package and in it were two beautiful old Chinese vases. I said, "Mr. Yee—these are too valuable. I couldn't accept them." He said, "I want you to have them." I asked why. He told me, "Mrs. Wicks, I have been in this town for ten years and you are the only one who ever called me Mr. Yee. And now I am going back home. They won't let me bring my wife and children here and I miss them too much, so I am going back to China. The vases are all I brought with me. I want you to have them." There were tears in his eyes as he said good-bye.

In my grandmother's arms, I cried my heart out for poor Mr. Yee. That was long ago—the defining moment when I learned respect for all people, the defining moment that would stay with me, would shape my life with passion for diversity, for inclusion.

Years later, January 15, 1998, I was at the White House, seated in the East Room, about to receive our country's highest civilian award, the Presidential Medal of Freedom. I was overwhelmed that day—I am still overwhelmed. In the front row before a low stage, I sat with other honorees including David Rockefeller, Admiral Zumwalt, James Farmer, Dr. Robert Coles, and Brooke Astor. Each of us had a military aide to escort us to the podium when our name was called. When it was my turn President Clinton ended my part of his citation by saying, "I will ask this pioneer for women, diversity, and inclusion to please come forward." As I walked toward the president, I remembered my grandmother and Mr. Yee and the defining moment of respect for all people, for diversity and inclusion—that moment in the mountains of western Pennsylvania that helped shape my life, that "determined the person I would be, the leader I would become."

Today, in the darkness of our times when we observe the lowest level of trust and the highest level of cynicism, the call for leaders who are healers and unifiers must be heard. Wherever we are, whatever our work, whatever our platform or forum—and we all have them, from the water cooler to the stadium—we must find the language that heals, the inclusion that unifies. It is a critical time for leaders at every level to make the difference. "For if the trumpet give an uncertain sound, who shall prepare himself to the battle," should be a powerful reminder for all of us.

In the future it will not be the one big message, the one big voice, but millions of us, in our own way, healing, unifying, and experiencing that one defining moment when we recognize that sustaining the democracy is the common bottom line—whoever we are, whatever we do, wherever we are, the call is to sustain the democracy.

Sometimes when we hear that call, we can go back in our own family history and recognize a connection, a force that moves us toward the defining moment.

So we each count those defining moments of our lives that defined the person we would be, the leader we would become. We find moments in our lives when someone helped to "shine a light" that would illuminate our future and the lives of all we touch.

This article originally appeared in *Leader to Leader*, Issue 45, Summer 2007.

Peter Drucker's Light Shines On

This is the column I hoped never to have to write—the column that would mark the moment we said goodbye to Peter Drucker.

We have lost the quiet, powerful intellect, the warm and generous friend. Peter redefined the social sector, redefined society, redefined leadership and management—and gave mission, innovation, and values powerful new meanings that have changed our lives.

I've had the privilege of sitting at the feet of Peter Drucker since 1981, participating in the founding of the Peter Drucker Foundation for Non-profit Management, being one of those fortunate few who, in 1990 and for the next 12 years, could listen and learn from him as he attended Drucker Foundation board meetings and conferences, participated in our video conferences, and advised in the development of our tools and books and videotapes. His philosophy permeated every aspect of our Drucker Foundation/Leader to Leader Institute initiatives, and will continue to do so.

When I learned of Peter's death, I was speaking at a conference in Tampa, so I returned to New York and flew to California in time to attend the small, private memorial service at St. John's Episcopal Church on Monday afternoon, November 14, in LaVerne.

Doris Drucker, their four children and six grandchildren, Bob and Linda Buford, John Bachmann, Claremont Graduate University representatives, old friends, and I were part of the small group of 25 who gathered to celebrate his life. The Druckers' son Vincent, their daughter Cecily, and John Bachmann spoke; there was the liturgy, and the service ended with a quiet, moving singing of "Amazing Grace."

On May 12, 2006, there will be a great celebration of Peter Drucker's life at the Claremont Graduate University.

I remember when I took my first professional position as executive director of Talus Rock Girl Scout Council in Johnstown, Pennsylvania, long ago in 1970. As I walked into the office that first morning I had under my arm a copy of Peter Drucker's *The Effective Executive* for each member of the staff. I had no idea who he was. I just knew his book was exactly right for our work. Six years later when I was called to New York to become the national executive director, CEO of the Girl Scouts of the USA, *The Effective Executive* traveled to New York with me, as did every book Peter had ever published.

Perhaps if I share with you how I met Peter and the influence he has had upon my work, it may be one more story to add to the thousands of how Peter influenced, encouraged, and challenged leaders to be leaders. All of us treasure his wisdom so generously shared.

I met Peter in 1981 when as CEO of the Girl Scouts of the USA I was invited by the chancellor of New York University to join 50 foundation and other social sector presidents for dinner, to hear the great Peter Drucker speak. I knew that in such a large group I would not have an opportunity to meet him, but I would have the opportunity to hear him live—Peter Drucker, the great thought leader who had influenced the volunteers and staff in the largest organization for girls and women in the world.

The invitation was for a 5:30 P.M. reception at the University Club in New York to be followed by dinner and Professor Drucker's address. Now, if you grow up in the mountains of western Pennsylvania, 5:30 is 5:30, so I arrived promptly at the University Club, only to find myself at the reception alone with two bartenders.

I turned, and behind me was a man. Obviously, if one grows up in Vienna, 5:30 is 5:30. The man said, "I am Peter Drucker."

Startled, I responded with, "Do you know how important you are to the Girl Scouts?" He said, "No, tell me."

"If you go to any one of our 335 Girl Scout Councils, you will find a shelf of your books. If you read our corporate planning monograph, and study our management and structure, you will find your philosophy," I replied.

Peter said, "You are very daring. I would be afraid to do that. Tell me, does it work?"

"It works superbly well," I replied. "And I have been trying to gather up enough courage to call you and ask if I may have an hour of your time, if I may come to Claremont and lay out before you everything you say the effective organization must have in place. We do. And I'd like to talk with you about how we take the lead in this society and blast into the future."

Peter replied, "Why should both of us travel? I'll be in New York in several months and I'll give you a day of my time." And that was the beginning of eight years of the remarkable adventure in learning and exploration the Girl Scouts were privileged to have with the father of modern management.

The great day came in the spring of 1981 when Peter Drucker met with members of the Girl Scout National Board and staff for the first time. Thus began a remarkable journey for us as he helped us answer those Five Drucker questions:

What is our mission?

Who is our customer?

What does the customer value?

What have been our results?

What is our plan?

I can hear his voice: "If you don't end up with a plan, a good time was had by all, and that is all." The auditorium of the Girl Scout Edith Macy Conference Center at Briarcliff Manor, Westchester County, New York, is named for Peter Drucker.

When I left the Girl Scouts of the USA, January 31, 1990, I bought a home in Easton, Pennsylvania, promised a publisher I would write a book on mission, and wasn't going to travel so much. But in mid-March, six weeks later, Bob Buford, Dick Schubert, and I (all of us enormously influenced by Peter in our careers) flew to Claremont to brainstorm a way to permeate the nonprofit sector with Peter's works, his philosophy. The day before Peter was to join us, we brainstormed all afternoon and evening and the result was the Peter Drucker Foundation for Nonprofit Management, a foundation that would deal not in money but in intellectual capital, and that would move the Drucker philosophy across the nonprofit world.

The next morning Peter arrived to meet us not knowing what we were up to. Newsprint covered the walls of our meeting room, and we took turns presenting our wonderful brainchild. Peter listened with no expression; we couldn't tell what he was thinking. Finally, "We will not name it for me. I am not dead yet and I do not intend to be an icon." (He lost that battle.) "We will not focus on me; there are a lot of good people out there and you will bring them in." (Already he had expanded our vision.)

Bob said that he and Dick thought I should be the chairman of the board. After all, I had just left the Girl Scout position and would have time to chair several board meetings a year for the new Drucker Foundation. Peter's response: "You will not be the Chairman, you will be the president and CEO and run it or it won't work." So six weeks after leaving one of the largest voluntary organizations in the world, I found myself the CEO of the smallest foundation in the world, with no staff and no money, just a powerful vision shared with co-founders passionate about bringing Peter to the wider world, transforming a sector that soon Peter Drucker would name "the social sector" because he believed it is in this sector that we find the greatest success in meeting social needs. The rest is history, well documented and alive on our Web site (www .leadertoleader.org), in our 20 books in 28 languages traveling around the world, and in this journal.

It is difficult to think about Peter without remembering his gracious manners, the power of civility that was so much a part of who he was and how he did what he did, a "gift of example." He was enormously generous with his time and his counsel. After that first transforming day with the Girl Scouts, he gave us several days of his time for the next eight years, just as he would pour his time, energy, and wisdom into the Drucker Foundation for the next twelve years. We learned about passion for the vision, the mission, from Peter, and thousands of our members, authors, and participants shared it with a new kind of exuberance as we documented his impact, his influence.

There are many of us who walk around remembering and trying to live up to his expectations of us: "Think first. Speak last." We remember how at Drucker Foundation Board meetings he would sit quietly, listening to every word, and then at that magic moment respond with the Drucker insight, and in a few powerful sentences clarify the issue, broaden the vision, move us into the future. Honoring the past but intensely defining the future was one of his great gifts.

For example, he wrote that we would see the reunification of Germany when no one else was making that statement. When the day came and the reunification was taking place, he was asked how he could have predicted this. His reply: "I never predict. I simply look out the window and see what is visible but not yet seen." In our tenuous times, when few attempt to "predict" the future, that one statement of Peter's philosophy encourages and inspires those who would be leaders of the future to "look out the window" as Peter did and "see what is visible but not yet seen."

Each of us has our own stories; all of us are better for having our moments with this quiet, courteous giant who for a while walked among us, with more questions than answers, thinking first, speaking last, as he counseled us to do. From 1990 on, over the next twelve years, as the Drucker Foundation and then as the Leader to Leader Institute, there are hundreds of moments and messages we captured and treasure; yet for this column I should like to focus on his work and his messages about the nonprofit, the social sector, for he did redefine, bring new recognition, new significance to the social sector as the equal partner of business and government. We hear his voice: "It is not business, it is not government, it is the social sector that may yet save the society."

Some of us may remember his seminal article in the July-August 1989 *Harvard Business Review,* "What Business Can Learn from Nonprofits." (Some were sure it had to be a typo before they read the article, which turned on its head the old view of the nonprofit sector as somehow the junior partner of business and government.) But Peter said, "The best-managed nonprofit is better managed than the best-managed corporation."

Peter forced this voluntary sector "to see itself life-size," and he changed the face of the social sector. When Peter came to that first meeting with the Girl Scout National Board and management team, he told us, after thanking us for permitting him to be there, "You do not see yourselves life-size. You do not appreciate the significance of your work, for we live in a society that pretends to care about its children, and it does not." And then he added, "For a little while you give a girl an opportunity to be a girl in a society that forces her to grow up all too soon."

Three years ago I was writing about children at risk and I called Peter and asked, "In 1981 you said, 'We live in a society that pretends to care about its children and it does not.' Do you still feel the same way?" Silence, then, "Frances, has anything changed?" Always Peter distilled the language until the message connected. Short, powerful, compelling. We never forget his words, and his message about our children grows in intensity.

He lived to see the vast proliferation of college and university non-profit management programs, centers for social enterprise—hundreds across the country and the world. And we can hear his voice, "Management is a liberal art." One last area of massive influence, of the many we could list, is his achievement in bringing business leaders to see the community as the responsibility of the corporation: "Leaders in every single institution and in every single sector . . . have *two responsibilities.* They are responsible and accountable for the performance of their institutions, and that requires them and their institutions to be concentrated, focused, limited. They are responsible also, however, for the community as a whole."

One measurable result of how Peter inspired leaders across the sectors to collaborate for the greater good is that collaboration, alliances, and partnerships across the three sectors, building the healthy community that cares about all of its people, became the powerful shared vision of principled corporate leadership and their social sector partners.

On our 15th Anniversary, April 2005, we celebrated Peter Drucker's life and contribution at our "Shine a Light" dinner. "Shine a Light" was appropriate that evening, and is now, for that's what Peter did for 95 years. His light illuminates the darkness, inspiring young people just discovering Peter, our young leaders of the future who are finding relevance and inspiration just as our leaders of the present have found this Drucker philosophy the indispensable companion for their journey. For the Leader to Leader Institute it is not enough to "keep his legacy alive." Instead, we will bring new energy, new resources, new partnerships to our new challenge. Peter's light shines across the sectors, reaching leaders hungry for Peter's messages that will illuminate, will change their lives, and in the end will move them to define the effective executive, the leader of the future. That will be the living legacy of Peter Drucker: vibrant, alive for a new generation, with new relevance, new challenge, new significance, new celebration of Peter Drucker's life, his influence, his light that shines anew.

This article originally appeared in *Leader to Leader,* Issue 40, Spring 2006.

Seeing Things Whole

ocus on the bottom line is drilled into many potential leaders who then lose their way on the journey toward significant and effective leadership. Certainly leaders need to manage the financial aspects of the organization with great effectiveness, but if we do not see the enterprise whole—including passion for the mission, values that are embodied in all we do, the customer who is listened to, partners whose collaboration is essential for our work, and a vision of the future that shimmers in the distance—we fail. Pulling out one piece, one action, one aspect of the leadership challenge is like playing a one-string guitar—noise but not much music.

Peter Drucker admonishes us to "Focus, focus, focus" (he never says it once). "Focus, focus, focus" drives us to pay attention to those few things, those critical initiatives, that determine relevance, viability, and success in the future—and this reverberating phrase walks around with many of us. Yet it does not negate the imperative of seeing the organization whole. Indeed, we can see the significant priorities clearly only when we see the organization complete and intact, embedded in the world at large. Only by seeing things whole can we understand and articulate to others *why* we focus on our few significant priorities. And only by seeing things in their entirety can we recognize when continued relevance and viability demand that we *change* our priorities.

When we see the organization whole and when our goals, objectives, and actions describe in a powerfully inclusive, embracing way the future we will bring alive, then all within the walls as well as those we serve beyond the walls and those future customers we will find, listen to, and serve will partner with us in our journey. All of this integrated wholeness—everything building upon everything else, flowing to and from in a circular movement—becomes a remarkable strategy for ensuring organizational relevance far into the future.

From Hierarchy to Wholeness

It becomes increasingly difficult to see things whole in the old hierarchy. People in boxes, squares, and rectangles find it difficult to move easily across the organization, in teams and groups, all carrying their own share of the big picture. More and more leaders are moving the enterprise away from the old boxes, into meeting the challenge of "managing in a world that is round" (*Leader to Leader*, Number 2, Fall 1996). Seeing the organization whole, flexible, fluid, and circular moves us into the community of the future.

Recently I have been inspired by two real, live examples of great leaders of vastly different organizations who both see the organization whole. One is Secretary Roderick Hickman, a Cabinet member on Governor Schwarzenegger's California team. Secretary Hickman is responsible for prison and parole reform in the California prison system, a system with more people incarcerated than are incarcerated in any other state in our country, and with a high recidivism rate. In a powerful California performance review of state agencies resulting in clear and inspiring direction for the future, Roderick Hickman has instituted a new philosophy and new "moving beyond the walls" initiatives with clear missions and goals for his agency. He believes in short, powerful mission statements. Quoting Peter Drucker he says, "It should fit on a t-shirt." So his mission for a new, powerful, cross-sector collaboration is, "To bring social sector organizations into prison and parole reform."

This is not just rhetoric. On January 26 I found myself speaking in Sacramento to 300 California social sector leaders and 100 corrections leaders in a day-long conference called "Bring the Social Sector into the Corrections Transformation." The interest, appreciation, and commitment were palpable. I left feeling moved and inspired—400 leaders were seeing a tremendous problem whole and finding ways to collaborate in a powerful partnership that will reform corrections, change lives, and transform communities.

The second example is very different. Richard Carrión is chairman and CEO of Banco Popular, which has branches in Puerto Rico and across the United States. Banco Popular is on *Fortune* magazine's 2005 list of 100 best companies to work for. Richard Carrión looks at the whole picture; he sees his bank not just as a highly profitable financial institution but also as a partner with organizations in all three sectors—supporting community projects, funding the documentary *DreamMakers*, seeing the community whole. An inspired leader and his people have embarked upon a transformation, taking banking officers out of the boxes of the old hierarchy into a strategic circle of clarity, innovation, and inclusion—circular management in action.

Seeing challenges, fostering community involvement and collaboration, and focusing on future relevance and significance bring these two very different institutions and their leaders into that small and inspiring band of leaders of the future who are leading from the front in helping to redefine the community, the society of the future. These leaders who see the organization, the community, and the society whole will in the end sustain the democracy. That's the big picture of seeing things whole.

Seeing Life Whole

In the end, seeing things whole is not just the imperative of business, government, and social sector leaders; the overarching, overriding imperative of seeing things whole rests with you and me. Seeing our lives whole is an even greater challenge than seeing our world of work whole.

How many times do we hear and talk about work-life balance, finding the delicate balance of family, friends, the people we love and who love us, and the colleagues who share our passion for the mission of the enterprise we lead and help lead? And then there's that other, further dimension, where we try to make a difference, work to change lives in the organizations we choose to serve, and volunteer in community efforts to move beyond the walls and build the healthy, inclusive community that cares about all of its people.

Add rock-climbing, tennis, 20 laps around the pool, running through Central Park at dawn, and we carry a big basket. How do we balance our lives in this miraculous wholeness with rich and varied dimensions of family, friends, colleagues, careers, service, physical and psychic energy, and spiritual and intellectual calling?

I remember the early days of the Drucker Foundation when I asked Lewis Platt, then chairman of Hewlett-Packard, to write an article for our book *The Organization of the Future*. One might expect this great leader in the field to write about cyberspace, the technology of the future. Instead, his response was, "If you don't mind, I would like to write about employee work-life balance, the greatest challenge to American corporations. And if we ever get it right, it will be win-win for everyone."

I've never forgotten our conversation. I carry his response around with me as I try to find the answers to work-life balance, to seeing life whole.

It is sad when highly successful corporate leaders tell me they were so busy making it that they really didn't have time for their own children, but now they are having a wonderful time with their grandchildren. That isn't good enough. For the leaders who read this journal, for the great thought leaders who think with us and write for us—for all of us—our joint challenge is seeing life whole, wherever we are on our journey. By thinking together we can find some guidelines.

In my last annual Adventure in Excellence seminar with 500 Girl Scout council CEOs and national staff members in late 1989, as I was about to leave that remarkable organization, Peter Drucker, Warren Bennis, John Work, and Marshall Goldsmith were the faculty. The last session had been billed as a dialogue with Peter and me but turned out to be something very different. The staff had changed the closing. I was to be interviewed by Peter Drucker. That was about as intimidating as anything one could imagine. But, as always, an encounter with Peter Drucker changes one's life, one's outlook, one's approach, in some measure.

At the end he asked me a question that each one of us should think about. How would you answer this question? "In a few months when you have left this organization and they hang your portrait on the wall, what do you hope that brass plaque beneath your portrait will say about you?"

Now, 500 remarkable fellow staff members were listening to what I hoped would be the message on the farewell plaque. I found myself saying, "I hope it will read, 'She never broke a promise.'" Peter Drucker said, "No. It will say, 'She kept the faith.'"

At the end of one career, or at the beginning of a new career, a new personal adventure, how do we balance all of the remarkable parts of our lives? We should have no illusions about competing interests, responsibilities, needs, opportunities, and that circle of people we love and who love us (and always beckoning in the distance, our vision of how we can serve, change lives, be an irresistible force for good wherever we go). We try to pack it all into one lifetime, one journey, one opportunity to see life whole and balance all of its irresistible parts. Seeing life whole, finding the balance, is the ultimate challenge. How well we respond will be recorded on that small brass plate under the farewell portrait—metaphoric or real.

This article originally appeared in *Leader to Leader,* Issue 37, Summer 2005.

The Art of Listening

The person who had the greatest impact upon my life, my career, and my work was my grandmother. People always expect me to talk about John W. Gardner, Peter Drucker, Warren Bennis, or Jim Collins—all the great thought leaders who have been part of my journey. They all have had a powerful impact upon my life and my work. Yet from my first consciousness of relations with other people my grandmother has been my leadership model. She listened very carefully. With grandchildren six or seven years old, she looked into our eyes and she listened as though it was the most important thing she could be doing at that moment, and she never cut us off. We finished our little story, whatever it was. And we learned to listen through our experience with her. She listened to us with total concentration and warm response and we learned to listen because we wanted to be like Mama Wicks. That kind of sensitivity and appreciation of others was a very important lesson, learned very early. And all through my life I often go back and think about something she encouraged me to memorize.

When she was a little girl, her family had a lumber mill back in the mountains of western Pennsylvania where they made barrel staves. The family built this little lumber mill long before the Civil War began, in the 1840s. Nearby was a one-room schoolhouse that she and her father and grandfather had attended. Above the blackboard was a maxim that could have been from a McGuffey Reader; it had always been there. It was this maxim she had me memorize: "If wisdom's ways you would wisely seek, these five things observe with care: of whom you speak, to whom you speak, how, when, and where." I memorized that when I was eight years old. Years later I have to smile; the only time I ever get into trouble is when I forget my grandmother's advice about "these five things."

I thought of my grandmother again recently when I was interviewed by a writer working on an article—on "the listening leader." Listening is an art. When people are speaking it requires that they have our undivided attention. We focus on them; we listen very carefully. We listen to the spoken words and the unspoken messages. This means looking directly at the person, eyes connected—we forget we have a watch, just focusing for that moment on that person. It's called respect, it's called appreciation, it's called anticipation—and it's called leadership.

Listening is one of the most effective ways of learning what the customer values. We listen to all our customers, all the people within the organization and those beyond the walls of the organization. And through listening we learn what they value. This is a critical skill and an indispensable attitude. When we learn this, it brings us to a higher level of understanding and appreciation of our own people and of those we can reach beyond the walls.

When we listen with total engagement, communication is not just saying something; it is being heard. And since communication is being heard, the leader consciously asks, "Am I getting through, is my message being heard?" How many times have we heard a leader complain, "I've told him and I've told him, but he just doesn't get it"? The leader was talking yet not being heard, was not communicating. When this happens, when it's obvious we're not being heard, it's time to listen, time to deliver the message a different way. Listening is the essential element of effective leadership.

How do we foster listening in others? Listening is not a solo performance, it is a connection—and is most successful when circular. I listen, you respond; you listen, I respond, and somehow in that magic circle of communication the messages are heard. The Great Stone Face is not exactly the most conducive face for good listeners; so we respond expressively.

Believing that the quality and character of a leader determine the performance and results, the success of our leadership depends on how effectively we mobilize our people around mission and values and vision, and how effectively all of our people listen to the customer. We are most successful when the communication is circular.

The writer interviewing me about listening asked what would be the one most important element, the one piece of advice I could share based on my own experience. Thinking of the management teams I've been part of, where positive feedback was key to growth and productive relationships, thinking through all the aspects of listening, of communication, rising to the top as number one was "banish the but." If we want people to listen, we must banish "but" from our vocabulary. How many times has someone told us how well we have performed—and we were feeling good about the feedback, listening carefully—then we have heard "but," and the positive, energizing part of the feedback was lost in the "but" and what followed it. "But" is nobody's friend—listener or speaker. "And" provides the graceful transition, the non-threatening bridge to mutual appreciation, the communication that builds effective relationships. Replacing "but" with "and" is the best advice I could give to the leader who listens and wants others to listen with an open mind.

There is another kind of listening—listening to our inner self. Listening to the whispers of our lives is critical. If we don't listen to the whispers of our lives, we miss many messages. I have written elsewhere about three kinds of whispers (see "Putting One's House in Order," *Leader to Leader*, Number 16, Spring 2000). First are the whispers of the body, when our body tries to tell us that something is not quite right. The more intellectual we are the more we tend to ignore the whispers of our bodies. Then one day an illness emerges and we can go back to that day when there was this whisper and we blocked or ignored it. And then there are whispers of the heart, of all the people we love, who love us, of our relationships. There are the whispers of the spirit, however we define our faith, that inner spirit, the spirit within—those quiet whispers that can comfort, heal, inspire.

The whispers of our lives are very important. When we ignore them our lives are diminished. We never reach the levels we could in understanding ourselves or in strengthening our relationships with others.

As I finish this column the future is ever more tenuous. I think again of my grandmother who, even as she listened to her children and her grandchildren, told us stories about the men in the family who went off to the Civil War and stories about their wives who were left behind to take care of children and farms. She talked in such a compelling way that we listened and remembered her stories long, long after she was gone and we were grown. (She left a treasure of Civil War letters and diaries for those grandchildren who had listened to her tales of the seven Pringle brothers who fought in the Civil War. Recently a cousin, one of those fortunate grandchildren who had listened to his grandmother's stories and inherited family Civil War letters, wrote and produced a poignant play based on Philip and Mary Pringle's letters, "Soldier, Come Home.")

A world at war requires new levels of leadership from all of us wherever we are, in whatever we are doing. When times are difficult, the art, the discipline of effective communication, becomes even more essential, and listening is the key for leaders who would be heard. Those who practice the art of diplomacy will fail unless the art of listening is an indispensable part of their portfolio. Listening is part of the art of leadership: never more needed, never more essential for leaders of change— the indispensable companion on our journey to leadership.

This article originally appeared in *Leader to Leader*, Issue 29, Summer 2003.

PART II

Building and Sustaining Strong Organizations

The Key to Cultural Transformation

In times of great change, organizational culture gets special attention. Leaders issue calls for cultural change, stating: "We need a more entrepreneurial culture," or, "We must create a culture of accountability." If we could alter the underlying beliefs of our organizations, the thinking goes, our practices would surely follow.

But changing the culture of an organization requires a transformation of the organization itself—its purpose, its focus on customers and results. Culture does not change because we desire to change it. Culture changes when the organization is transformed; the culture reflects the realities of people working together every day.

Peel away the shell of an organization and there lives a culture—a set of values, practices, and traditions that define who we are as a group. In great organizations the competence, commitment, innovation, and respect with which people carry out their work are unmistakable to any observer—and a way of living to its members. In lesser organizations, distrust and dysfunction are equally pervasive.

If we note Peter Drucker's definition of innovation—"change that creates a new dimension of performance"—it is the performance that changes the culture—not the reverse.

When I was leading a transformation of one of the largest organizations in the world, with a workforce of over 700,000 adults serving more than 2.2 million young members, our focus was not on changing the culture—though that was a result. Our focus was on building an organization committed to managing for the mission, managing for innovation, and managing for diversity.

Changes in the practices and beliefs of an organization do not happen because someone sits in the executive office and commands them. They happen in the real world, in local communities. The 700,000 women and men who served as volunteers and staff, as well as the parents of the young people served, had to be deeply committed to the goal of equal access and to building a richly diverse organization.

We changed the very face of the organization—the program, the uniforms, the way we trained adults and delivered services, the way we communicated—but never the purpose, the values, the principles, or the promise of a great institution. The changes came through a mission-focused effort that was inclusive and involved those affected by the decisions as well as those implementing them. We listened to our customers—some of them only five years old.

A respected first-time visitor to our headquarters, listening and observing, said, "Rarely have I observed a culture that is so palpable." That culture flowed from the transformation—it changed as the organization changed.

Our passionate purpose was creating opportunities for girls to reach their own highest potential. We concentrated on building a viable, relevant, contemporary organization that truly furthered that purpose. Through that building process, the culture was inexorably changed. The result was the greatest membership diversity in 78 years, coupled with the greatest organizational cohesion anyone could remember. The culture became a powerful reflection of the organization and its people, those who served and those who were served.

From experience and observation, there are seven essential steps to transform a culture through a changed organization:

- *Scanning* the environment for the two or three trends that will have the greatest impact upon the organization in the future
- *Determining* the implications of those trends for the organization
- *Revisiting* the mission—answering Peter Drucker's first classic question, "What is our mission?" and examining our purpose and refining it until it is a short, powerful, compelling statement of why we do what we do
- *Banning* the old hierarchy we all inherited and building flexible, fluid management structures and systems that unleash the energies and spirits of our people

- *Challenging* the gospel of "the way we've always done it" by questioning every policy, practice, procedure, and assumption, abandoning those that have little use today or will in the future—and keeping only those that reflect the desired future
- *Communicating* with the few powerful, compelling messages that mobilize people around mission, goals, and values—not with 50 messages that our people have trouble remembering
- *Dispersing* the responsibilities of leadership across the organization, so that we have not one leader, but many leaders at every level of the enterprise

And along the way, by initiating each of these challenging steps, leaders of the organization, in their behavior and language, embody the mission, values, and principles. By working with others toward change, we create the desired result—the inclusive, cohesive, productive organization reaching new levels of excellence in performance and significance.

Peter Drucker, in *Managing in a Time of Great Change*, makes a powerful statement: "For the organization to perform to a high standard, its members must believe that what it is doing is, in the last analysis, the one contribution to community and society on which all others depend."

That is the marriage of culture and organization, of belief and practice, that marks our best institutions. And in a wonderfully circular way, as the organization and its people grow and flourish, the culture reflects and resounds and delivers a message—changing as the environment and the needs of our customers change.

In the end, it is a good thing that culture is not easily changed. A culture defines the heart of the organization, and a change of heart is not to be taken lightly. But the introspective and inclusive process by which an organization formulates its values and revisits its mission will enable organizations to serve their customers and communities with high performance, to be viable and relevant in an uncertain future. That capacity to change and to serve is the essence of a great and vibrant culture.

This article originally appeared in *Leader to Leader,* Issue 12, Spring 1999.

Leadership by Example

Twenty years ago, when the Peter Drucker Foundation for Non-profit Management was founded, an exuberant Peter Drucker led the way toward an adventure in significance. The Foundation, now the Leader to Leader Institute, continues to be faithful to Peter and his philosophy. Only the name has changed.

In November 2001, Peter Drucker wrote "A Survey of the Near Future: The Next Society" in *The Economist*. The article was full of Peter's wisdom, such as "I never predict. I simply look out the window and see what is visible but not yet seen."

The most important observation in the article is one I've been carrying around with me for about ten years. It is on change agents:

> To survive and succeed, every organization will have to turn itself into a change agent. The most effective way to manage change successfully is to create it. But experience has shown that grafting innovation on to a traditional enterprise does not work. The enterprise has to become a change agent. This requires the organized abandonment of things that have been shown to be unsuccessful, and the organized and continuous improvement of every product, service, and process within the enterprise (which the Japanese call *kaizen*). It requires the exploitation of successes, especially unexpected and unplanned-for ones, and it requires systematic innovation. The point of becoming a change agent is that it changes the mind-set of the entire organization. Instead of seeing change as a threat, its people will come to consider it as an opportunity.

"Changing the mind-set of the organization" continues to be the enormous opportunity (not challenge), and innovation and planned abandonment are even more urgently required.

It is amazing and gratifying that even at the close of Peter's 100th birthday celebration all over the world, his wisdom and his philosophy are bringing new understanding to leaders of "the next society."

I met Peter Drucker in 1981, when I was CEO of the Girl Scouts of the USA, and for the next eight years, he gave us two or three days of his time each year and made an enormous and positive impact upon our work and success.

The next year, 1982, a young man from California walked into my Girl Scouts office at 830 Third Avenue in New York with a gift. Marshall Goldsmith had developed a 360° feedback process and wanted to give it to our organization. He would use it with my management team and me; he would help train facilitators and we would move Marshall's 360° feedback across the organization. It fit perfectly with our corporate management plan for the future, and we began our second adventure with a great innovator.

I left the Girl Scouts of the USA on January 31, 1990, and my last year was the most exuberant of my 13 years with the best organization and best people in the world. Six weeks later, I found myself the president and CEO of the new Peter F. Drucker Foundation for Nonprofit Management, with Peter as the honorary chairman and Marshall Goldsmith as a member of the board.

Leadership on the World Wide Web

We are deep in webinar excitement. Now if you had suggested a "global webinar" in 1990, the reply would have been, "global yes, but webinar?" Not so today. On August 10, 752 participants from 37 countries and over 400 companies and organizations took part in the "Leadership by Example: A Conversation with Frances Hesselbein" webinar, the online global leadership gathering and conversation in which I was the speaker. From early on in the event, participants were asking questions, sharing thoughts on our virtual walls, and reflecting on the experience itself, and the responses continue to come in, with requests for repeat or follow-up global webinars.

A few comments about our webinar:

"This was an extremely beneficial experience. It was not only informative, it was a dynamic way to interface with the content of what you shared. Being part of a global session brought with it an uncommon synergy or coherence that seems to me to be quite a phenomenon in itself. Intuitively, I felt an exceptional connection, which I had not expected. What a brilliant use of media! Thank you for the effort put into this event."

"Thank you for the very inspiring conference this evening. I believe you mentioned a quote from one of the participants which started with the invisible red line . . . It was in connection to leaders and the fact that his invisible red line never breaks . . . I firmly believe that we all eventually will connect with those who we are destined to meet during our journeys."

"I want to thank you for an engaging and thought provoking webinar today. It was truly a great experience. I watched and listened to it with a few members of my new leadership team and we then had some good dialogue on their ideas around the key messages. It was a small (but important) step in helping us become a stronger and more cohesive team. Thank you for the opportunity."

The "Leadership by Example" webinar was designed and produced by Debbe Kennedy, the founder of the Global Dialogue Center, as her contribution to moving our work around the world, a great gift to leaders everywhere. I found it intriguing that the first two countries to sign on were Pakistan and Kenya; 35 others followed. Debbe and I decided that rather than charging the usual $8 or $10 per person, there would be no charge, so that money would not limit participation by leaders in some countries and some groups. To have so many organizations sign on, some with multiple sites, was gratifying, and equally gratifying were the responses coming during the webinar and in the open half-hour that followed. It was so successful that now leaders are asking, "What's next?"

Readers can access the "Leadership by Example: A Conversation with Frances Hesselbein" webinar at our Web site: www.leadertoleader.org.

Celebrating Our Shared Journey

As I write this in late September, the Leader to Leader Institute's calendar for the balance of 2010 has two celebrations. On October 11, Marshall Goldsmith, one of the world's greatest executive coaches and the author of *Mojo: How to Get It, How to Keep It, How to Get It Back If You Lose It*, and a new book to come, will receive the Leader to Leader Institute's fifth "The Leader of the Future Award" in New York City. Alan Mulally, president of Ford Motor Company, was our first awardee in 2006, followed by Andrea Jung, president and CEO of Avon Products, in 2007; A. G. Lafley, recently retired chairman of the board, president, and chief executive officer of Procter & Gamble, in 2008; and General Eric K. Shinseki (U.S. Army Retired), now the Secretary of Veterans Affairs, in 2009.

The final Leader to Leader Institute celebration of 2010 will be our annual Holiday Reception on December 16 on Mutual of America's wonderful 35th floor in New York City. This year in a small gift bag for each guest will be an early copy of my own book *My Life in Leadership: The Journey and Lessons Learned Along the Way* (official publication date January).

In just two days, Alan Mulally, our first "Leader of the Future" awardee, will go to West Point with me to engage cadets in a leadership dialogue. I wish you could be there to appreciate the response of these cadets to a great, principled, ethical, and incredibly successful corporate leader, a model for us all; Alan's four "Ford Goals" and West Point's "Duty, Honor, Country" will get along very well.

I will continue to be at West Point monthly until my two-year appointment to the Class of '51 Chair for the Study of Leadership ends in May 2011. Each time I meet with a class of cadets, I bring with me a great thought leader and the two of us begin the dialogue. Then the cadets dive into the dialogue in the most profound and stimulating way. Their questions and comments will give Alan Mulally a new kind of energy. I'll share it. And then, at lunchtime in that great hall, 4,400 cadets and faculty will give the president and CEO of Ford Motor Company an appreciative, high-volume welcome he will never forget and always cherish. They too will remember the day a corporate leadership icon traveled to West Point, honored to join the newest members of that "long gray line."

There is a long and powerful list of fellow travelers who have shared our journey—400 who have written for our books and *Leader to Leader* journal, spoken at our conferences, served on our board, and traveled with me when we went abroad to China, Poland, Korea, and South Africa. Whenever they get the call, they respond. The generosity of these friends of the foundation/institute is what has enabled us to end our 20th year with exuberance and great optimism. There are not only books, journals, conferences, seminars, and monographs, but also the whole new world of the Internet—the global webinars, the Innovation of the Week, and a great Web site of the future. Please visit it.

Peter told us in 2001 about the next society. Today, ten years later, we look ahead at this generation's "next society." Global webinars are only the beginning. Together we will chart the new journey to significance.

If the above sounds a little "bookish," I guess it's only natural for us now that we are publishing our 28th book. Our books have now been published in 30 languages. We'll have a special celebration when we hit "30 books in 30 languages"! You will be part of it.

Our 20th anniversary brings back years, experiences, and dreams shared with fellow travelers. Thank you for sharing our Drucker Foundation/Leader to Leader Institute journey. Now for the next 20!

This article originally appeared in *Leader to Leader*, Issue 59, Spring 2011.

The Inspiring Journey We All Share

I had a wonderful husband. John was a writer, a newspaper night city editor right out of journalism school, and a filmmaker who made wonderful documentaries and was one of the first six Robert Flaherty Fellows (Robert Flaherty was considered the father of the modern documentary—his films include *The River* and *Nanook of the North*).

We had one small problem. He took a cool, clinical, measured look at things, while I would want to leap ahead. "Wonderful. Let's go!" I'd say, and on and on. One day when I was particularly exuberant (obnoxious) about a possibility, John said, "Frances, if you were drowning and going down for the last time, you would be shouting, 'Today was great, but tomorrow will be better.'" That became the family joke.

But keeping our spirits up and seeking out hope in tough times isn't a joke, it's essential. In these uncertain times, we cannot give in to despair or cynicism.

Every day, if we look, if we seek them out, we can find moments that give us hope. "Lowest level of trust, highest level of cynicism" in our own society may be what we are observing, hearing, feeling at times. Yet positive messages, trends, and examples are all around us, led by this "Crucible Generation" and all of us who recognize, support, and cheer them on.

Here is one example. On May 22, I attended the West Point Graduation, Class of 2010, where President Obama gave the stirring commencement address. It was inspiring and respectful, combining the gratitude of our country with great expectations of these young second lieutenants, commissioned officers at the end of the ceremony. This was the first time that two women finished atop the graduating class in West Point's 208-year history—Alexandra Rosenberg and Elizabeth Betterbed. This year's class included 136 female graduates.

"The faces in this stadium show a simple truth," the president told the graduating class. "America's Army represents the full breadth of America's experience. You come from every corner of our country—from privilege and from poverty, from cities and small towns. You worship all of the great religions that enrich the life of our people. You include the vast diversity of race and ethnicity that is fundamental to our nation's strength.

"We cannot succumb to division because others try to drive us apart. We are the United States of America, and we have repaired our union, and faced down fascism, and outlasted communism. We've gone through turmoil, we've gone through Civil War, and we have come out stronger—and we will do so once more."

President Obama knows how important hope for the future is. After his speech, he gave out a number of the diplomas, and then shook the hands of all 914 graduates.

When I talk about today's Crucible Generation, it is not an abstraction. I have one of this generation in my own family—Johnny, in college, writing stirring poetry and stories, with his two-year-old daughter Isabella and wife Nicole as his cheering section. I remind him that he is the fourth generation of John Hesselbeins—all writers—and his own father, the third, tells him that of all four generations, he is the best.

Even though his father, my only son, is an invalid and cannot get out of bed, even to sit in a wheelchair, he does not despair. While he was in the Army, scar tissue had to be removed from his lungs. Today, spending 24 hours on oxygen and with congestive heart failure, John says, proudly, "I was a soldier, I am a soldier, I will always be a soldier." (Isabella, the baby who adores him, is what is keeping him alive, says his doctor.)

"Today was great, but tomorrow will be better" was our family joke, but it expresses an attitude that is essential to living a life with purpose. Why should we not be positive? And add Claire, Doug, Gloria, Justine, Risa, Theresa, the young and energetic Leader to Leader staff, plus the remarkable board, led by Fred Altstadt, chief operating officer of Mutual of America, to my working life, and it is very difficult to be anything but filled with gratitude, expectation, and a sense that for all of us, it's never just a job. Every day is a gift.

I'll close this column with a moving experience I had at the Women Presidents' Organization in Fort Lauderdale.

The day before, I'd been at Fort Benning, where I spoke to General Michael Ferriter's U.S. Infantry Maneuver Center of Excellence and his officers, and received the Saint Maurice Medal, one of our U.S. Army Infantry's highest awards. I am now an honorary member of the U.S. Infantry, and the award ceremony was one never to be forgotten. The plaque with the inspiring medal hangs in my office at West Point, a reminder of one of the great days in my life.

From there, I went to another "fort"—Fort Lauderdale to speak to 500 women who all own their own businesses, the Women Presidents' Organization. (I was gratified to learn that 95 percent of these business owners had been Girl Scouts.) One of the most moving experiences happened at the end of my speech to the group. My speech, "Leadership Imperatives," was exceptionally well received, with standing ovations and some tears at the end. After the speech, I left the stage and went down on the floor to mingle with these business leaders.

We expressed appreciation for each other and shared lots of hugs. Then before me stood a young woman from another country, probably somewhere in Asia. She knelt before me, on one knee, with hands clasped, head bowed, and said, "Bless me. Please bless me." I come from a long line of Methodist ministers, but nothing in my background ever prepared me for this moment.

I looked at this earnest young woman, placed my hand on her bowed head, and said, "May all the blessings be yours." She rose, embraced me, in tears, and then I saw behind her, kneeling on one knee, her colleague, who also said, "Bless me, please bless me." I placed my hand on her head and said, "May all the blessings be yours." It was a rare and moving moment for me. And for the leaders who surrounded us.

One more moment to be grateful for—never to be forgotten, always to be remembered on this inspiring journey we all share.

This article originally appeared in *Leader to Leader,* Issue 58, Autumn 2010.

An Antidote to Cynicism

When a university student and a cadet at West Point ask me the same question, months apart, I have to think about why. Different times, different places, different circumstances, yet the same question: "What makes you so positive?" "Why are you so positive, all the time?"

My reply begins with a somewhat flippant, "Well, you see, even my blood type is B-positive!" Then I go on to explain the "why" I am "so positive." I tell them, "In my whole lifetime, in my own country I see the lowest level of trust, the highest level of cynicism, yet I am filled with hope for the future of our people, of our country." Then I go on to tell them why. I talk about this generation now on campuses, at our military academies. This is a different generation from some earlier ones—far less cynical, more committed to serving, to making a difference. A recent *USA Today* study found that even though jobs are scarce and money is tight, it has not stopped this generation from helping others. Young adults who grew up in the shadow of the 9/11 attacks, saw the wreckage of hurricane Katrina, and searched for jobs during a recession are volunteering at home and abroad in record numbers.

For some time, I have been ending speeches to college and university students, cadets at West Point, and just last week to cadets at the U.S. Air Force Academy in Colorado Springs, "Ten years from now may they say of you, 'the future called and they responded. They kept the faith.' Then twenty years from now they will say of you, 'Once again, the greatest generation.'" This has been my passionate belief, based on hundreds of encounters with this generation of college and university students, military academy cadets, and U.S. university students attending the Oxford Conclaves on Global Ethics in England.

As I have related in a recent column ("A Lifelong Commitment" in *Leader to Leader,* Number 55), the University of Pittsburgh Hesselbein Global Academy Summit participants reached a new high in civic and social engagement in July 2009. July 2010 will find us back at the University with 25 university students from all over the world, 25 students from universities across our country, and 13 mentors equally represented. I expect the same positive powerful engagement, the commitment we experienced in July 2009, with this new Summit of 2010.

April began with the third "Leadership Dialogue" at West Point, part of my Class of '51 Chair for the Study of Leadership program. Margot Tyler of the Bill and Melinda Gates Foundation and I shared our Leadership Dialogue with cadets, and then Margot spoke to a larger group of graduates, friends, cadets, and faculty at the gathering. I gave the closing speech to West Point's 11th Annual Conference on Diversity. Three days at West Point in April and every moment positive and inspiring.

My next Leadership Dialogue will be in September with Alan Mulally, the President of Ford Motor Company. The cadets will be ready with their questions and a warm welcome.

All of these adventures provide a powerful antidote to cynicism. As I walk on university campuses, the grounds of the U.S. Air Force Academy recently, and West Point every six weeks, I find new energy and new hope from this generation.

Tomorrow I fly to Fort Benning to speak to our Army officers based there, then on to another fort, a very different one, Fort Lauderdale, Florida, where Marshall Goldsmith and I will present a dialogue on "The Imperatives of Leadership." With Marshall's "Life is good" approach to life, "be positive" will permeate the day.

And yet I remember the question a student asked after my speech at another university a few years ago: "Why should I not be cynical?" I tried my best to respond with all the positive reasons, yet I am not sure I succeeded. I asked him to "stay in touch" but I never heard from him again. His question haunts me and I try, in speeches to other university students, to give real-life examples of positive initiatives in all three sectors that are addressing the challenges of our times—not theory, these examples have names, faces, documented results. Regular readers will remember their stories from many of my earlier columns.

For 20 years, the Peter F. Drucker Foundation for Nonprofit Management—now Leader to Leader Institute (only the name has changed) has tried to be a force for good, sharing awards, publications, and services with leaders and organizations in all three sectors, always sharing a positive view of the future and its possibilities. Peter Drucker's philosophy, his work, his ten years as our honorary chairman inspired us, motivated us, and challenged us, and his influence is as powerful today as it was in 1990. We remember his profound wisdom: "It is not business, it is not government, it is the social sector that may yet save the society."

Our 27 books in 30 languages bring positive, powerful resources to leaders in all three sectors. The Leader to Leader Institute's newly redesigned Web site (www.leadertoleader.org) carries video clips—Mark Thompson's major contribution—featuring our Leadership Dialogues with great thought leaders and great corporate leaders—Jim Collins, Alan Mulally, Sir Richard Branson, Keith Ferrazzi, Darlyne Bailey, the Dalai Lama, Marshall Goldsmith, and others.

We can make a difference in these uncertain times. So as I observe, work, and engage with our new chairman, Fred Alstadt, the Institute's Board of Governors, and the best executive staff team (which shares the board's commitment), two words describe the next two years: Bright Future. No wonder my B-positive genes are showing that the very challenges of our times bring even greater opportunities to serve for all of us, in all three sectors.

This article originally appeared in *Leader to Leader*, Issue 57, Summer 2010.

Changing Hearts, Changing Minds— Changing Lives

Harvard Business School turned 100 years old this year. I was happy to accept an invitation to speak on the morning of the day-long celebration, which ended with a great party on the lawn in a giant white tent. On our panel were two other leaders: Johann Olav Koss, one of the greatest winter athletes of all time—a four-time Olympic gold medalist in speed skating—and Nancy Barry, the former president of Women's World Bank, now with Inter-American Development Bank.

I often ask people, "What do you think was the subject the three of us were invited to speak on?" Everyone guesses something about leadership and management (after all, it is a business school). They are as surprised as I was to learn the topic we were asked to address: "Changing Hearts, Changing Minds." I added "Changing Lives," for that is what we do when we change hearts and minds. Each of us was invited to share in five or six minutes a story of an action we took in our own careers that changed hearts and minds.

As I read the invitation I knew the story I wanted to share. It happened when I served as CEO of the Girl Scouts of the USA, and it involved Harvard Business School faculty members. It is documented in a Harvard Business School case study and in the lives of millions of Girl Scouts.

In July 1976 I left the mountains of western Pennsylvania to become CEO of the Girl Scouts of the USA—the first national executive to come from the field, from within the organization, since 1912. It was the largest organization for girls and women in the world, 650,000 men and women serving 2.25 million girls. The organization had lived through the trauma of the '60s and the early '70s, but the program had not changed in 12 years and the organization was ready for a transformation. The world had changed.

We were determined to become highly relevant, to take the lead into the future. Our hearts hungered for change, but how could we change minds, become a highly contemporary, highly effective organization of the future—changing lives in this changing society?

Our remarkable people produced remarkable results. In one year, with the help of four distinguished educators, we created a new, highly contemporary program for girls—heavy on math, science, and technology. Computer Fun became the most popular proficiency badge. And we quickly more than tripled racial and ethnic membership and strengthened minority participation on the national board, on my management team, and in 335 councils across the country, creating a richly diverse cohesive organization.

But even with these impressive achievements, I realized we had not fully changed hearts and minds. As I worked with the 335 Girl Scout Council CEOs, the indispensable team, I was aware that some did not see themselves life-size. If they did not see themselves life-size, how could they see the organization and the future life-size?

So two and a half years into the transformation, we went to Harvard Business School to talk with Dr. Regina Herzlinger about the possibility of a team of business school professors developing a Corporate Management Seminar for Girl Scout executives, just for us.

She immediately saw the value of our proposal and, with Dr. Jim Heskett and several other professors, designed the most powerful executive development seminar for 335 local council CEOs and 100 national staff members. Our people participated—50 at a time—until all had completed the Harvard Corporate Management Seminar for Girl Scout Executives, and each had a Harvard certificate to hang in their office, with new spirit, new appreciation, high motivation. Some 500 hearts, minds, lives were changed.

Now when you make available this exposure to great academic leaders in the perfectly designed leadership development opportunity, you ignite a revolution of rising expectations. So, they asked, "What's next?"

These were the CEOs responsible for a cookie sale that generated a third of a billion dollars every year; they were responsible for hundreds of conference centers, camps, headquarters buildings, impressive budgets.

So "what's next" became Dr. Herzlinger's "Asset Management Seminar"—an enormous contribution to the effective financial management of a great organization.

With this investment by a team of Harvard Business School professors in the development of the key professional leaders of a great movement, membership soared—the adult workforce grew from 650,000 to 788,000, and racial-ethnic membership more than tripled, changing hearts, changing minds, changing lives throughout the Girl Scouts of the USA.

What was an indispensable ingredient, the initiative in this massive transformation of the largest organization for girls and women in the world?

It was the major investment in the leadership development of our key professional leaders, and having the best business school faculty in the world to partner with us. An interviewer once asked me, "What led you to choose Harvard Business School faculty?" My reply, "It's simple. Only the best is good enough for those who serve girls."

Telling that story was my contribution to a great 100th Birthday Celebration. Isn't it amazing how circular life can be?

After that first round of professional leadership development programs, Peter Drucker himself provided a similar opportunity at Claremont University for the 335 Girl Scout Council Chairmen and the National Board.

Changing hearts and minds means changing lives. We remember Peter Drucker advising us that "the bottom line of every social sector, nonprofit organization is changing lives." Sometimes when I've used this quote from Peter Drucker with corporate leaders, some will say, "The bottom line for our company is changing lives, as well. The services, the products we deliver change lives." And frequently, corporate leaders share the remarkable success they are having with their own corporate social responsibility projects. A few years ago, it was not the usual response. Today it is, and the success is dramatic, the results measurable.

Since then, I have been to Grapevine, Texas for the Military Child Education Coalition 10th Annual Conference, with the theme "For the Sake of the Child, for the Good of the World," with 800 military officers from all five branches and their spouses. They met working to support the 1.8 million children of our military, children going to schools all over our country, all over the world. Some move frequently, some have both parents serving in the military. If you want to be inspired, go to the Military Child Education Coalition Web site and see some of the artwork of these children. "My father, my hero" is the caption on one watercolor portrait of himself and his father by a seventh grader whose father is serving far away.

The opening session touched our hearts and our minds as Lieutenant Colonel Greg Gadson, his wife Kim, and two teenage children came on stage, Colonel Gadson in a wheelchair. Both Colonel Gadson and Kim Gadson are graduates of West Point, class of 1989.

In May 2007, Colonel Greg Gadson, Commander of the Second Battalion, 32nd Field Artillery, was returning from a memorial service for two soldiers from his battalion when he lost both his legs to a roadside bomb in Baghdad. Currently assigned to the Army's Warrior Transition Brigade, Colonel Gadson told us, "It's not about what happens to you in life. It's about what you do about it." As husband and wife talked about their lives, the family's lives they are living today, duty, honor, courage, and love were palpable. Real people, real lives, real courage. Later in an afternoon in a Distinguished Lecture breakout session Gabby Gadson, age 17, and Jaelen Gadson, age 15 led in "Living in the New Normal: A Kid's Perspective," with a West Point faculty facilitator. The children were as moving and inspiring as their parents.

Dr. Darlyne Bailey, Dean of the College of Education & Human Development at the University of Minnesota, was the first keynote speaker and her opening presentation on preparing our children to be the leaders of tomorrow set the perfect tone for what followed. Jim Collins opened the second day of the conference with a powerful keynote address that moved everyone in the audience to a new level of appreciation of the messages of *Good to Great* for the military and its families. No one will forget his passion, his energy, his message.

General William E. (Kip) Ward and I had a "Fireside Chat for Military Leaders" on improving the academic lives of military children. We included "learning about the social sector as a means for significant change." General Ward is the Commander of the new United States Army Africa Command. He and his wife Joyce are passionate advocates for the care and education of the children of our military.

Once again I had the privilege of serving with a great leader—General "Kip" Ward—who changes hearts, minds, and lives, including mine.

This Military Child Education Coalition, caring for the schoolchildren of the military, is serving in the most caring and responsive way that underscores our theme—Changing Hearts, Changing Minds, Changing Lives. I've never had a greater honor than being part of this program, which permits me to work with military officers and spouses and makes me realize ever more deeply that "to serve is to live," as these military families work to make the best of separation and stress. No complaints, ever—they serve with pride and dedication and their children reflect the family's "Duty, Honor, Country" values. "To serve is to live."

This article originally appeared in *Leader to Leader*, Issue 50, Autumn 2008.

Emerging Leaders

With all the dissonance and the lack of consensus in our turbulent society, there is one clear area of agreement—emerging leaders are in the spotlight, at the head of the line, everybody's baby. It is fascinating to listen, read, and explore this intense interest in a leadership cohort emerging in all three sectors.

Great authorities are writing and speaking about emerging leaders. Theories abound: Generation X, Y, and Z. Corporations, organizations, agencies—enterprises large and small—are working intensely to identify their own emerging leaders and design learning opportunities and other programs for them.

Not all agree on a description of emerging leaders, yet there is agreement on the significance of these young leaders in redefining the future of the organization, of the society. One of the exciting parts of my life these days is the number of invitations I receive to dialogue with small groups of these young men and women. And I'm finding their questions far more exciting than my responses. This is a different generation, and whether it is the recent Columbia University MBA class, or the 13 young women who are leaders from the Lehigh Valley of Pennsylvania hosted by the Women's Leadership Initiative of the United Way who visited me in New York, there is common language, common ground. These are some of the questions they ask:

How did you get started?

When did you know you would be a leader?

Where do you get your energy?

How do you elevate others while accomplishing your mission?

How do you find a mentor?

How do you get into the social services profession as a career?

How do you find a community project?

What was the most difficult moment in your work with the Girl Scouts? Describe a bad day.

To that last question, I replied, "I never had a bad day in those 5,000 days (13-plus years) I served with Girl Scouts of the USA. I had some tough ones, but never a bad day."

Managing for the Mission, for Innovation, for Diversity

In all the groups I meet with and in e-mail I receive from emerging leaders around the country, there is enormous interest in values, how you live them, and what to do if you are expected to violate your own principles in the workplace. "To serve is to live" is not a foreign language to these young leaders. They are volunteering, serving in amazing ways—not waiting until they are 50 to begin to change lives, including their own.

What encourages me most, personally, is emerging leaders who are passionate about learning more about "the father of modern management," Peter Drucker. Drucker Societies are being formed all over our country and the world. The power of his work is appreciated now more than ever by these young leaders.

I recently joined the New York City Drucker Society in its monthly evening session to talk about Peter Drucker, his work, his philosophy, and our partnership with him as we formed a foundation devoted to nonprofit management in 1990.

I told them the story of meeting Peter Drucker quite by accident in 1981, when I had been with the Girl Scouts of the USA for five years and in that period, those remarkable 650,000 men and women serving 2.5 million girls had transformed the organization. Their story intrigued Peter and for the next eight years he studied us, wrote about us, and gave us two or three days of his time each year. I explained that six weeks after leaving the best people and the best organization in the world, I found myself with Bob Buford and Dick Schubert, all three of us Drucker disciples, founding the Peter F. Drucker Foundation for Nonprofit Management (now the Leader to Leader Institute) and serving as its first president and CEO. Smallest foundation in the world, with the greatest vision—moving Peter Drucker's work around the country and around the world.

And who were among our most responsive customers? Young leaders, who would sit at the feet of Peter Drucker wherever we gathered. Our publications, visual materials, and teleconferences reached them. These emerging leaders became part of this great intellectual adventure, "an adventure in significance."

When we talk about leaders of the future managing for the mission, managing for innovation, managing for diversity, young leaders like those I met at the Drucker Society will take the lead in embracing all three as essential if the enterprise is to be the organization of the future.

They Are the Future

Ten years ago, we published *The Leader of the Future,* which Marshall Goldsmith, Richard Beckhard, and I edited. Think about the world of our leaders in 1996–1997. That world is gone forever.

Ten years later, for our emerging leaders as well as leaders of any generation, there is a new *The Leader of the Future 2* for leaders in a new age, living with enormous change and ambiguity. Our emerging leaders of 2008 will find and use the resources that will support them as they redefine the future. And in October, the Leader to Leader Institute will publish *The Organization of the Future 2* with 25 great thought leaders, once again writing in the context of our own times.

I speak twice a week somewhere in our country, three times a year abroad. Last year Taiwan, New Zealand, Australia; in 2008, I will go first to South Africa in April, Norway in June, and China in November. And I spend a third of my time with corporations, a third with social sector organizations, and a third on college and university campuses. Something amazing and wonderful is happening. Wherever I go, I find a new generation of leaders, leaders at every level—mission-focused, values-based, demographics-driven. They see the future because they are the future, as hard as it is to define.

This is where I find my hope—on the campuses of colleges and universities, at West Point, with graduate students who are working full time, taking classes at night or Sundays. I've discovered that this is a new breed, a new generation, different from several earlier cohorts. In the darkness of our times, they "shine a light," as Jim Collins would say.

Why We Do What We Do

Last week students from a research project at Kennesaw State University came to New York to visit with us at Leader to Leader Institute, spending several hours in a provocative, illuminating dialogue (I listen more than I speak), and then we had lunch together with more conversation. Whether it is those young leaders who are women working with Mack Truck, Air Products, Just Born, United Way, Boys and Girls Club, Wachovia, the Lehigh Valley, the Kennesaw students from Georgia, or an MBA class at Columbia Business School, they bring a special quality to the exploration that gives me hope for the future. These emerging leaders are the future, and I am blessed to be part of their adventure in learning.

When the Women's Leadership Initiative group from the Lehigh Valley came to New York, I invited Michele Hunt to join us for the dialogue. She is the author of *DreamMakers: Putting Vision and Values to Work*—and was Max De Pree's legendary "vice president for people" at Herman Miller—not vice president for human resources or personnel, but vice president for people.

So Michele and I were the team for the Women's Initiative dialogue and it was far more stimulating for these young leaders to have a team—Michele and me—than one of us alone.

And all of us, leaders of the present, appreciate the privilege, the imperative of mentoring these emerging leaders. I mentor three. Eight years with a New York University graduate student from China, whose parents I met in Schezen. Ten years of mentoring a young Coast Guard officer, now in the corporate world; and on occasion, a young lawyer from the South. What do I learn from this experience with these three young women? That mentoring is circular. I learn as much from them as they do from me. Mentoring is a leadership privilege.

I make time to meet with young leaders who want to come to 320 Park Avenue just to talk, to connect. And sometimes they introduce me as their "mentor." I'm not that in the strictest sense, but we are "fellow travelers," sharing the journey. Gloria Fahlikman, my indispensible executive assistant, always finds time on our overstretched calendar for these young leaders who, for a brief moment, remind us of why we do what we do.

We will be hearing and reading much about "emerging leaders" in the months to come. However defined, however engaged, we'll be supporting them, cheering them on, and, in the end, following them, for they are our leaders of the future.

The emerging leaders I encounter are sending a powerful message of leadership, of building trust, of ethics in action, of the power of diversity, of inclusion, of courage, of celebrating the intellect, of leading from the front into an uncertain future. They send a powerful message. And my message to them is, "We look to you to take the lead, leading beyond the walls, a model of ethical global citizenship, an example of the power of education. As William Butler Yeats wrote long ago: 'Education is not the filling of a pail, but the lighting of a fire.' You light a fire."

This article originally appeared in *Leader to Leader*, Issue 49, Summer 2008.

The Indispensable Partnership

Our times are teaching us a lesson about the indispensability of effective governance and management in all three sectors—corporate, social, and government. Daily headlines and nightly newscasts deliver tragic stories of failed leaders—chairmen, presidents, CEOs—unfaithful to mission, oblivious to fiduciary responsibility, disrespectful of the workforce, and disdainful of the stockholders' and the public interest.

After the shock and disbelief that we feel with each disclosure—and as the list of failed and failing corporations, organizations, and public agencies grows longer—all of us who serve on boards or lead the management of an organization ask, "What is our company, our enterprise doing today to prevent the betrayal of trust tomorrow?"

Questioning Governance

Reading this, we may think only of headlined corporate scandals, yet this crisis crosses all three sectors. Nonprofit organizations and the institutions of government carry their share of this burden. We are learning bitter lessons from the failures of flawed leaders and indifferent boards. The litany is long—of board members who are unaware or indifferent to dubious financial practices, who are ignorant of salaries, benefits, loans, who do not ask the critical questions or request clarification or additional information required for informed decisions.

In these times, wise leaders in all three sectors no longer blithely agree to serve on a board without asking serious questions. A few years ago, this might not have been the case; today it is essential.

I've just finished a week at two board meetings and a keynote speech at a national conference. And in a few weeks I'll be serving on the Women in Corporate and Not-for-Profit Governance Panel at MIT's Sloan School of Management for women who have decided that one of their responsibilities to the community is to serve on boards of directors of corporations and social sector nonprofit organizations. I find it fascinating that these remarkably able women—graduate and undergraduate students, MIT Sloan Fellows, women admitted for next year's MBA class, and Sloan alumnae—are engaging in a governance roundtable where several of us (including Judy Lewent, CFO of Merck, Madeleine Condit from Korn/Ferry, and Ilene Gordon from the French company Pechiney) will be speaking from our own experience and philosophy on the governance of organizations and the responsibilities of boards of directors.

When I speak to the Sloan School students and alumnae I am going to share a list of questions every potential director should ask:

- *What is the mission of the organization?* The response should be why it does what it does, the organization's reason for being. If there is no mission statement, or the response focuses on the what and not on the why it does what it does, say good-bye.
- *What is the board's vision of the future?* This question should bring an illuminating response. No vision, no acceptance. Some visions of the future are so compelling, we sign on almost before we go down the list of questions a prudent potential board member asks. Others make it simple to decline.
- *Is there a positive partnership between the chairman and the president or CEO?* The board should see the president as the partner of the board, not as a subordinate. A positive partnership here provides a model for the board as a whole and for the enterprise.
- *Does the president or CEO appreciate and observe the clear and sharp differentiation between governance and management?* The demarcation between governance and management is critical, with management not attempting to establish policy, and the board not attempting to manage the organization.
- *Is this a learning organization?* Look for continuing leadership development opportunities for both board and staff.
- *Are the corporation's most recent audit and yearly financial reports and annual report delivered along with the invitation to serve?* Read them carefully before you accept. If they're not provided, decline.

- *What is the climate at board meetings?* Check for comprehensive background material, energetic engagement, and full disclosure before action is taken.
- *Does the board, as Peter Drucker advises, see the president as "the hinge to the board"?* Other members of the management team should not have private relationships with board members, creating power pockets that can diminish and divide.
- *Does the organization have directors and officers insurance?* This is essential in these litigious times.
- *What does the organization hope I will contribute as a new board member?* And ask yourself as well what you will bring to this board that will further the mission, enhance the results.

These are just some of the questions that may be raised in our roundtable at MIT's Sloan School to a group of women who will make exceptionally effective board members. They understand management in all its dimensions and will relate the best practices they have learned about the enterprise, corporate or nonprofit, they will serve.

Beyond these questions, a clear understanding and commitment to planning/policy/review (PPR)—the three major, generic areas of board responsibility for all enterprises—are essential:

Planning. The board has the responsibility for strategic planning, establishing mission and goals and reviewing these every two to three years against an environmental scan that helps the board identify major trends and their implications for the future of the organization.

Policy. The board determines all policies that the organization must adhere to—policies on salaries, benefits, and other compensation, as well as policies involving partnerships, alliances, collaboration—all need to ensure that objectives and action steps presented by management will achieve the goals and further the mission of the corporation or organization.

Review and oversight. This third critical responsibility demands careful study and understanding and approval of all management actions and reports, including acceptance of the audit and financial reports; approval of changes in direction, mission, and goals; the annual performance appraisal of the president or CEO with a review of the preceding year and acceptance of the president's goals for the new year.

The PPR approach carried out in good faith by board members who took their governance responsibilities seriously would have prevented the sad ending of careers and the failures of too many companies and organizations. An awareness that board members are the custodians of public trust and money and carry a tough fiduciary responsibility is part of the exciting dialogue we engage in when asked to serve on a board of directors, knowing it could be a great adventure in civic responsibility.

Exemplary Board-CEO Partnerships

Fortunately, beyond the headlines of the moment lie thousands of powerful partnerships of the chairman and the president, the board and management, that meet and exceed the ethical, responsible standards and expectations of public trust, public money, public support. Let me share several experiences.

I began the week mentioned earlier by chairing the meeting of the National Board of Directors of Volunteers of America, one of the country's oldest (107 years) human service organizations, with "there are no limits to caring" as a reminder of its identity. Before the board went into session, the board and management team spent a half-day examining critical issues as background for planning and review. As a group, we continue to do this periodically, to ensure that we are aware of emerging trends and issues that will have the greatest impact upon our work, upon those we serve.

The president, Chuck Gould, and I try to model the essential partnership that must be effective, just as the total board, the management team, and those of us in the field must see ourselves as effective partners if we are going to be viable, relevant, and faithful to our mission in the future. Chuck and I try to observe "the philosophy of no surprises," a powerful concept for a chairman-president partnership that is open, stimulating, and, we believe, productive, with total trust and mutual appreciation. It was a great meeting.

The next day, I went from Coral Gables and Volunteers of America to Boca Raton where Mutual of America Life Insurance Company was holding its board meeting. I have the honor of serving on this great corporate board, where the partnership of Chairman Bill Flynn and President and CEO Tom Moran is as powerful as the partnership of its board and management. Theirs is a model of openness, energetic engagement of the distinguished board, total transparency, and a clear vision of the future of the organization.

I ended the week with yet another organization with a name ending with "America," speaking to the National Corporate Leadership Conference of Girl Scouts of the USA. This was the first time I've spoken to the chairmen and presidents of 300 Girl Scout Councils and the national board and staff since I left that remarkable organization in 1990 as its CEO.

My last year with the Girl Scouts, the year of leadership transition, was the most exuberant of my whole career. So it was a moving experience to stand before these remarkable leadership teams and once again be part of a culture, a cohesion, and a commitment that I expressed in the opening sentence of my speech, "You can leave the job; you never leave the Movement." At the end, they presented me with the Woman of Distinction Award and I said good-bye to "the best organization in the world, the best people in the world," in my own slightly biased opinion.

The most illuminating part of that day was the presence and performance of that new leadership team, Cynthia Thompson, the chairman, and Kathy Cloninger, the new CEO. They represented the kind of leadership team every organization, corporation, government agency deserves—passionate commitment to mission, to innovation, to diversity, to building the cohesive, inclusive organization that helps each girl to reach her own highest potential.

On-the-Ground Inspiration

In one week, I found inspiration in three examples of the power of the partnership of governance and management, the chairman and the president. Two were social sector nonprofit organizations, one a corporation, yet all three shared common language, common ground, common bottom line of changing lives and building community. I carry lessons learned from these great organizations wherever I go—not the theory of governance and management, but shared experience, deep involvement, and critical observation.

This balances, for me, the tragic stories of companies and organizations that betrayed public trust, failed themselves and their workers, their shareholders, their stakeholders. For all over this country are hundreds of thousands of corporations and social sector organizations that strive and succeed in building the quality of governance, management, and results our institutions and the public they serve require and deserve.

So next month when I go to the Sloan School of Management's gathering of women eager to serve in yet another way, as committed, ethical, productive members of our country's boards of directors, across the sectors, it will not be theory of governance I will be delivering. It will be the inspiring story, the on-the-ground story of principled, mission-focused, values-based organizations with high performance and measurable results I encounter all over this country.

This article originally appeared in *Leader to Leader,* Issue 33, Summer 2004.

Crisis Management: A Leadership Imperative

Crisis management is not a discipline to be learned on the job, in the midst of the storm. It must be learned and practiced when there's not a cloud in the organizational sky. Now, more than ever, examples of crises badly managed in all three sectors underscore the imperative of preparing for a crisis that may lie ahead, that may never happen, that even so must be anticipated by responsible, effective leaders.

There are too few outstanding examples of leaders who understood the imperative, who prepared the organization for an emergency, who instilled values that would support a powerful and ethical response, and who—when the crisis hit—led from the front and communicated in an open and powerful way. These few prepared when the sky was blue and took costly action—a wise investment, actually—that protected the public and, in the end, the good name and the future of the enterprise.

In the end, crisis management is a test of the quality and character of leaders as much as it is a test of their skill and expertise. Organizations that cope well with crises have put their houses in order; they know what their values are and have a well-articulated mission that permeates the organization. They know what they stand for. Crises can strengthen these organizations, even as they undermine—or destroy—those that do not know what they stand for. Even in a crisis, leadership is a matter of how to be, not how to do it. Yet there are still steps that wise leaders will undertake.

Probably the most positive and successful example of managing a crisis with total success is the way James E. Burke and Johnson & Johnson handled the Tylenol crisis in the early 1980s. When it was over, Jim Burke was an icon and Johnson & Johnson a celebrated corporation. His is a case study of what happens when a corporate leader—guided by the beliefs and values that define the culture of a great corporation—communicates with clear and forthright messages, reassuring the public and the people of the corporation. Today, despite predictions at the time that Tylenol was a fatally wounded brand, it is still one of the top-selling over-the-counter drugs in the country. John Joseph of the Wharton Center for Leadership and Change says, "Johnson & Johnson's corporate credo—overseen by top management but mastered by all—steered the company successfully through its Tylenol crisis in 1982 and continues to serve as a compass by which the organization guides itself today." Johnson & Johnson's management of the Tylenol crisis continues to be the standard against which many observers measure the management of the long line of current crises that are part of the landscape in all three sectors.

A more recent example of powerful and successful crisis management came on September 11, 2001. The world watched heroes—firefighters, police officers, medical personnel, and rescue workers—respond to the unimaginable disaster. Skills they learned and practiced in hundreds of different crises prepared them for the ultimate challenge. The many teams became one team, and their enormous courage, passion, planning, preparation, and total commitment inspired the country and the world. They gave us the ultimate example of crisis management on a massive, global scale, and the lessons learned from their response to September 11 apply to whatever crisis leaders may face on any scale in any organization. Some of us who have had the uncoveted experience of managing a crisis in a complex and far-flung organization know from that experience there are some essential steps to be taken by an organization, regardless of size or sector, long before disaster strikes.

A crisis management team needs to undertake a study of every possible crisis that could hit the organization, and develop a scenario for the response to each one. This list of possible crises coupled with the responses required for each takes time and investment, but it is the best disaster insurance we can have. This study is kept in desks, on computers, in easy reach of every member of the crisis management team. Once the plan is ready, the training and preparation for implementation takes place.

Some organizations have the expertise within the enterprise to train and prepare their people for that dark day—should it come. Other organizations may choose an outside consultant to assist in this demanding management responsibility, the training of those who will lead the response.

Even if, as some of us have personally experienced, the crisis that hit was not on the carefully prepared list of possibilities, the principles are the same, the plan of action works, and the results are positive even though the crisis has a different face from all those we brainstormed. Here are my steps to effective crisis management:

- Appoint a crisis management team.
- Brainstorm all possible crises that could hit the organization; develop the response required for each.
- Prepare a master plan everyone understands, a plan with clear delegation of responsibility across the organization.
- Designate the official spokesperson at every location, or the one voice for the organization.
- Prepare the field as carefully as headquarters—one team, one voice, one response.
- Secure or activate the best public relations team.

When lightning strikes, mission, values, and integrity in managing and communicating will be the crucial ingredients to a successful conclusion. Effective leaders will regard communications within the organization and with all constituents as just as important as those with the public and the media. They will communicate with integrity and openness, using messages consistent with mission and values. And they will stay close to the customer, both internal and external, focusing on what the customer values.

Recent history, as well as lessons of the past, places crisis management as an inescapable challenge to all leaders. In 2002 there is a greater urgency, a clearer recognition that crisis management is a leadership imperative. Perhaps at one time it could have been part of Plan B. Today it is not debatable. Every dollar and hour spent in preparation, before the fact, is an indispensable investment required for future confidence, credibility, and relevance. Leaders of character will be ready.

This article originally appeared in *Leader to Leader*, Issue 26, Autumn 2002.

PART III

Leading Today and Tomorrow

The Leaders We Need

As this winter issue of *Leader to Leader* is being prepared for publication, we face an abrasive political campaign in a country divided and in the midst of war. By the time this issue is published, the campaigns will have ended and the country will know who its president will be, but the divisions will remain. Healing the wounds will be one of the challenges to leaders everywhere.

This is a time of testing for leaders as well as a time for a new kind of courage—the courage to lead in a time of great divisiveness. In an earlier issue of *Leader to Leader* (Number 20, Spring 2001) and on our Web site (www.l2li.org/leaderbooks/l2l/spring2001/fh.html) is a checklist for an organization's relevance and viability—*When the Roll Is Called in 2010*. Now is the time to develop our checklist for leaders of the future who embody the values, principles, and philosophy needed to lead from the front, right into this turbulent future, in a world at war. Added to the leadership qualities we look for in every sector, the leader as a healer and a unifier ought to be high on our leadership checklist. Whether we are leading in a corporation, a government agency, or a social sector or non-profit organization, we need to ask, What kind of leaders do our people deserve and require in these demanding times?

We need leaders who practice dispersed leadership, leaders at every level of the enterprise, so that we are relying not on *the* leader but on leaders dispersed across the organization—on ourselves. These are leaders who remember Peter Drucker's admonition, "They're not employees, they're people."

We need leaders who believe and embody in concept, language, and action that leadership is a matter of how to be, not how to do, knowing in the end it is the quality and character of the leader that determines the performance, the results.

We need leaders who believe and demonstrate that the people of the organization are the organization's greatest asset—making that a reality, not a slogan. These are leaders who build the richly diverse organization with powerful representation at every level, on all teams, in all groups, on all boards, in all management, and in all visual materials. They realize that rapidly changing demographics present enormous opportunities.

We need leaders who help distill the concept and language of the mission—why the organization does what it does, its purpose, its reason for being. These leaders invest in building the mission-focused, values-based, demographics-driven organization, permeating the total organization with mission and values, and demonstrating the power of reflecting the many faces of our country.

We need leaders who communicate with the people of the organization, the customers of the organization, and the many publics we engage—always reflecting in our communications that "communication is not saying something, communication is being heard." Here the act of distilling language is one of the most effective skills the leader of the future can perfect. One sentence, one paragraph, one page—connecting, helping, inspiring, being heard.

We need leaders who practice the art of listening, who practice Peter's "think first, speak last." Leaders who are healers and unifiers use listening to include, not exclude—building consensus, appreciating differences, finding common concepts, common language, common ground.

We need leaders who in their own lives try to find work-life balance and make work-life balance a reality in the lives of their people. If you think that this is a lovely ideal but not realistic in today's tough world, try comparing the productivity and morale of a workforce that is encouraged and supported in finding this rare work-life balance with those of a dispirited workforce where work-life balance is not a consideration and "take no prisoners" is a valued management style.

Perhaps most of all we need leaders who share successes widely while accepting responsibility for shortfalls and failures. These leaders take a tough measure of their own performance, aware that their language, behavior, and action are measured against their self-proclaimed values and principles.

Tonight as I write this column I think of the difference in our society and the world since our last general election. September 11 had not yet changed our world. It was a different world, not a world at war. While the basic qualities of leaders that corporations, government agencies, and social sector organizations need remain constant, some of them may have new significance, may move up the list in importance because of our times and the new testing we face.

We are all challenged to lead in an era of discontinuity far greater than 10 or 20 years ago. So all of us try to be prescient in a rapidly changing world, as we try to peer into that future no one can describe with certainty. We try to describe the world of the future—try "to see what is visible but not yet seen," as Peter Drucker says, against the backdrop of our times. Only then will we be able to describe the qualities of the leaders we will need in the years ahead.

Are there qualities needed now more than ever, whatever the organization, the sector, as we move into 2005–2010? I propose that this is a time for leaders of quality and character, leaders who live the values, who are healers and unifiers, who bring hope to the people and the work of the enterprise. Bringing hope, healing, and unity within the organization and beyond the walls are essential qualities our times require of our leaders of the future.

This article originally appeared in *Leader to Leader,* Issue 35, Winter 2005.

1964 | New Delhi, India | FH as Chair, International Conference of the World Association of Girl Guides and Girl Scouts.

All photographs have been printed with permission from the Frances Hesselbein Leadership Institute.

January 15, 1998 | East Room of The White House | First Lady Hillary Clinton welcomes FH to the White House, where she was honored by President Clinton with the Presidential Medal of Freedom, the nation's highest civilian award.

1986 | Washington, DC Ritz-Carlton | FH with First Lady Nancy Reagan, whom the Girl Scouts honored with the first "Say No to Drugs" badge.

July 13, 2009 | Pittsburgh, PA | 50 global student leaders gather at the University of Pittsburgh for the Inauguration of the Hesselbein Global Academy for Student Leadership and Civic Engagement.

2010 | U.S. Military Academy at West Point | As Class of 1951 Chair for the Study of Leadership at the U.S. Military Academy at West Point, FH engages with West Point cadets in the Department of Behavioral Sciences and Leadership.

1964 | Poona, India | FH and Madame Lakshmi Mazumdar, president
of Girl Guides in India, welcomed by the second President of India,
Dr Sir Sarvepalli Radhakrishnan, while chairing the International
Conference sponsored by UNESCO and theWorld Association of Girl
Guides and Girl Scouts in New Delhi with college student Girl Guides
and Girl Scouts from all over the world.

New York, NY | As CEO of the Girl Scouts of the USA from 1976–1990, FH emphasized a message of inclusiveness and empowerment, while tripling minority membership.

1970 | Johnstown, PA | FH serves as the first woman to chair a United Way campaign.

1978 | New York, NY | FH and Halston, who had just designed the Girl Scout uniform.

November 2, 2009 | New York, NY | General Eric K. Shinseki, U.S. Army (Ret.), Secretary of Veterans Affairs, with President of Ford Motor Company, Alan Mulally and his wife, at the annual Leader of the Future Award dinner hosted by The Hesselbein Institute and Mutual of America Life Insurance Company.

Beyond the Distracting Clamor, We Hear the Leaders of the Future

Recently my autobiography, *My Life in Leadership: The Journey and Lessons Learned Along the Way*, was launched. My publishers, Jossey-Bass/Wiley, hosted a great reception in New York for 95 friends and colleagues at the Four Seasons Restaurant, and in that warm and friendly gathering we all became friends as if we had not met before.

I remembered the months and years of trying to write the book. Being as "personal and intimate" (my publisher's language) as I had to be turned out to be one of the most agonizing challenges of my life. It was not just revealing very personal experiences or explaining *why* I did something, not just the whats, that were challenging, but also wondering whether readers could have any interest in these stories of my life.

Well, it is finally out and the agony is over. Book reviews are up on a number of Internet sites and blogs, including this from a young man: "How long it took to read—90 minutes/3 reading sessions," "Favorite quotes: 'And when do we make the great discovery that leadership is a journey, not a destination.'" And finally, "My big idea from reading this book: The essence of leadership is presence." Another review on the Internet says, "As inspirational as it is practical, *My Life in Leadership* is filled with Frances Hesselbein's universal leadership lessons that will serve any leader, of any age, in any sector." And if you'll permit me to mention one more: "Strength and grace. . . . Those words sum up for me the essence of Frances Hesselbein and the quality of her leadership." I am humbled.

These comments are a backdrop to my observations in this column—all about leadership in a time of crisis. In speeches these days, I often say, "Today, we are finding the highest level of cynicism, the lowest level of trust in our own country in our own times." Instead of being intimidated by this reality, all of you—the leaders of the future—see new opportunities to lead in the very challenges that confront us. Peter Drucker's observation, "Good manners are the lubricating oil of effective organizations," seems to have been lost in the venomous attacks, the lack of respect in our dialogues across the sectors and within the organization. The language of respect, collaboration, common mission, common ground seems to be part of the past, yet I feel it is needed now more than ever. I believe we will soon see leaders using the language of reconciliation, of healing and unifying. Perhaps the noise of the present has been drowning out the voice of reason—the voice of the future that is still there.

I've shared with you before that where I find my greatest hope in our tenuous times is in the generation now on university campuses and at the military academies: "The Millennials," or as Warren Bennis calls them, "The Crucible Generation." From e-mail, questions, conversations before and after speeches, I am discovering that the leadership our country, our society, our people deserve lives in this new generation. With this reality of our leadership of the future, I challenge myself and all of us to take today's crisis in communication, crisis in leadership, crisis in collaboration in perspective. Our Crucible Generation is preparing to lead and we are their partners.

I often think of my own family, ancestors, generations from President John Adams, all our men on both sides who fought in the American Revolution and the War of 1812. I think of the seven Pringle brothers— ages 19 to 28—when Lincoln called, they all volunteered. And from my grandmother's trunk of Civil War letters, we know how wives, children, soldiers suffered, in their words, "to save the Union and free the slaves." Just one of millions of American stories of how our people met the crises, the opportunities of their times.

Today, "to serve is to live" is not a foreign language. The tide is changing and we will be asking, "Is this the language, the action, the direction that will help us in sustaining our democracy?" For underneath all the negative forces at work in the society is the reality of the shared and powerful future of our American democracy. The clamor may be distracting, but the dream, the vision is there. In the days to come, the voices of leaders will be heard—leaders of the future, across the generations, will take the lead.

This is my vision, as March comes in "like a lion," and the roars are deafening. By the time you read this, once again, March will have gone out like a lamb, and "Bright Future" is high on the agenda.

This article originally appeared in *Leader to Leader*, Issue 61, Summer 2011.

Together, We Can Change the World

Early in 2001, before September 11, Peter Drucker said, "The next ten years will be years of great political turmoil in many parts of the world, including the United States." Life was lovely in that bubble before September 11, and some people were puzzled by Peter's pessimism. How sadly prescient Peter's message was.

By the time you read this column, the election will be over and the United States of America will have a new president. A page will have turned—but the challenges we face will continue. Turmoil is not new to our people.

So what will we do in those early months of 2009 to heal and unify our people, our country? For it is the responsibility of each one of us to respond. Remember John W. Gardner's "Bugle Call Right in the Ear":

> "I keep running into highly capable people all over this country who literally never give a thought to the well-being of their community.

> "And I keep wondering who gave them permission to stand aside! I'm asking you to issue a wake-up call to those people—a bugle call right in their ear. And I want you to tell them that this nation could die of comfortable indifference to the problems that only citizens can solve. Tell them that."

One resource I keep with me is "A National Study of Confidence in Leadership," from the Center for Public Leadership, John F. Kennedy School of Government, Harvard University. On page 3 is the National Leadership Index 2007, with the question, "How much confidence do you have in the leadership of the following sectors?"

These are the six sectors with the highest level of confidence:

1. Military
2. Medical
3. Supreme Court
4. Educational
5. Nonprofit and Charitable
6. Religious

I happen to work in three of the six—nonprofit and charitable, educational, and military, frequently with the people of the U.S. Army, one of the richest parts of my life.

So, I'm in three theaters where I try to make a difference, for all three can heal and unify, and they do. And all of us can find our place in serving the common good in our way, making our own contribution to a new and vibrant and caring society that only citizens can restore.

In New York City, where our offices have been located since 1990, there are 1,000,000 schoolchildren—500,000 of whom will not receive a high school diploma. There will be no high school diploma, no job, no future, no hope for far too many of our children. And they are *our* children. And New York is just one example. Schools all over the country are failing our children. Building more prisons is not the answer.

"Comfortable indifference" is not for us, determined to sustain the democracy. For a long time I have lived by this philosophy: "Since the beginning of our country, two institutions have sustained the democracy. One is the U.S. Army—the military—the other is public education."

Today our U.S. Army is stretched and public education is failing millions of our children. Both are essential institutions. So we need to put the turmoil behind us and turn our attention to providing leadership in building the healthy community—taking our personal share of the responsibility. It would follow that if we fail in the support of our children in our schools, in the support of our young men and women in our military, we must ask the question, "How can we then sustain the democracy?"

That's the big picture. We know how to lead, to mobilize, to pursue, to contribute our own unique share to changing lives, building community, serving those who serve our country. But will we heed the call?

As the Old Testament reminds us, "If the trumpet sounds an uncertain call, who shall gird himself for the battle?" It can be an exuberant response, with all of us saying, "These are our children." If not all of us, some of us must take the lead. It's all about leadership, and knowing "to serve is to live." It's a new beginning for our society.

I write this before the election; you are reading it after the new president has been elected. The new president can give leadership in all the areas I have been sharing with you, but it will take all of us, in our many different ways, to build the new and healthy communities that provide a strong education for all our children, the caring for all our people. If this sounds too optimistic, would you like to list the alternatives?

You may ask, "With the needs so great, how do we begin?" Let's begin with our public schools, our responsibility for these, our children.

"Adopt a School" is not difficult. New York has a new organization, New York City Leadership Center, working to encourage local faith communities to adopt nearby schools. Sometimes, a church is just across the street from an urban school. Great results are anticipated.

I know of schools where the teachers are "maxed out" purchasing school supplies out of their own pockets. I asked one teacher in such a school, "Is there anything you need for Graduation Day?" He responded wistfully, "It would be nice if we could have two American flags for the kids to carry in the procession."

These are those seemingly small things a friend of a school can provide. We think back to the schools we attended as children—with adequate schoolbooks and supplies, American flags in every room, and assume it's the same world within those school walls today. For some, it is. There are wonderful schools in our country. But there are thousands of schools crying out for help as their children fail, drop out, and join the millions of "invisible children."

A little help—books for libraries, ink cartridges for computer printers, school supplies, career fairs, can change the lives of those children, their schools, their communities.

But soon it will be a new year, a new time, a new call to serve, to make a difference. Together, we can change the world, bring a new world to all our children. To serve is to live.

This article originally appeared in *Leader to Leader*, Issue 51, Winter 2009.

In Service to the Common Good

In 1998, General Dennis Reimer, chief of staff of the U.S. Army, and General Timothy Maude, deputy chief of staff for personnel, invited me to the Pentagon to speak on leadership and diversity to the officers responsible for Army personnel. After I spoke, we had a spirited dialogue, and then a general said, "I am responsible for recruitment. We aren't getting the number of new recruits we require. If you were in charge, what would you do?"

I took "in charge" broadly and replied, "Tomorrow morning, I would institute national and community service for every 18-year-old man and woman in the United States. They would serve 18 months or two years. They could serve in one of the five branches of the military, or communities across the country could design community service programs that would bring new levels of inclusion, diversity, engagement. They could work on the roads and bridges of the crumbling infrastructure of our country; they could move into our public schools and work in a teaching corps that would ensure that every child could read and double the number of our children receiving high school diplomas. And when their two years of service were completed, every young man and woman would be eligible for scholarships—for two years of college or technical training—whatever they desired.

"Our 18-year-olds would have found themselves, would be imbued with the spirit of service, and our country would have a new face, a new respect for all people. And all of our children would have an opportunity to learn and grow. That is my response to your question."

The general said, "That is the last thing I expected you to say." That was 1998. I wasn't "in charge" then nor am I now, but the needs of our schoolchildren and of bridge, waterfront, and road infrastructure are greater in 2007 than in 1998—and today the Army is stretched far beyond reasonable limits. (We lost General Timothy Maude when the plane crashed into the Pentagon, September 11. The next month, he was to open our Conference Board-Drucker Foundation Leadership Conference. General John Keane spoke at the opening and we dedicated the conference to the memory of General Maude.)

So how do we mobilize our communities, our leaders, our families—all of us concerned with the health of all of our children, the health of all of our communities, the health of our U.S. Army? For a long time I have believed that since the beginning of our country, two institutions have sustained the democracy. One is the public schools of our country. The other is the U.S. Army. Both need our passionate and generous support. Now, more than ever.

The health of our schools will determine our future. Yet we have recently learned that 50 percent of all minority children will not receive a high school diploma; 70 percent of all poverty-level children will not receive a high school diploma; and 30 percent of all American children will not receive a high school diploma.

For many people, these are invisible children. A powerful program of national and community service would institute such a mobilization of idealism, passion, love of country, and desire to serve (understanding that "to serve is to live"), that it could transform our democracy.

And our army is an essential institution in our democracy. In the midst of a long war, with an army with too few soldiers, extended tours, families strained, and long-cherished values in peril, it may seem naive to ask what this new army of 18-year-olds could do with this new vision of serving, making the U.S. military their own. It may be naive, but it is essential. It requires more than telling the story in a new way, communicating the message of love of country and service beyond self in new and powerful ways to all of our young people. It requires tangible action demonstrating that service to the U.S. military is indeed service to the *common* good.

When we truly focus on the common good, service is a privilege—not a chore but a remarkable opportunity. Inspire the brightest, most articulate 18-year-olds to tell the story and communicate the many ways to serve. Recruitment will have a new definition, service will have a new significance that comes from values, from the hearts our new message has touched. Here is where we find the new alliances, the new partners, the new collaborations that will inspire and support a new generation ready to serve, in the military, in our schools, restoring our roads and bridges, meeting the unmet needs across the community. All of this requires—from all three sectors—vision, courage, innovation, generosity, sharing, inclusion. Shimmering far in the distance is our vision of the future: a country with citizens who care about all of our people, and young men and women called, eager to serve leaders at every level sustaining the democracy.

Today, many of us have a forum, a platform. How can we use it to encourage, motivate, inspire 18-year-olds to volunteer? And how can we mobilize colleges, universities, foundations, citizens to say, "Yes. Two years of service, two years of the learning of your choice"? If we think this is too ambitious, too massive, someone else's business, we need to think again. The alternatives are not pleasant to contemplate.

In five or ten years, these hundreds of thousands of young men and women who served would go on to the next adventure in learning, and then become a new generation of citizens—citizens who have served their country, their communities, their people, and who will forever sustain the democracy.

I am finding my hope on college and university campuses, at West Point and others. There is something about this new generation of students that is different. They are volunteering wherever they are. I get e-mails from students wanting me to know how they are serving. Some end with our common language, "to serve is to live." Could it be possible that twenty years from now we will say, "Once again, the greatest generation"? All this begins with you and me—encouraging, supporting, inspiring, enabling today's 18-year-old men and women to see service in the military and our communities as the bright future for them and for every 18-year-old in our country.

In the darkness of our times, then, this new generation will shine a light illuminating the future our people yearn for and deserve.

This article originally appeared in *Leader to Leader*, Issue 47, Winter 2008.

Faces in the Crowd

Traveling twice a week, speaking here or abroad, lands me in many airports, with lots of waiting in long lines, yet I often see faces in the crowd that give me hope. Whenever I see one of our soldiers in uniform in an airport, I always go up and say, "I hope you understand how much we appreciate what you are doing for all of us and our country." Invariably, the reply is "Thank you, ma'am" or "Just doing my job." So many of our service people are so young, they touch my heart.

Recently I was in an airport, changing planes to go on to an engagement in the Texas Panhandle, where I was speaking the next day. Walking toward the gate, I noticed a very young soldier, went up to him and said, "Sir, I hope you understand how much we appreciate you and what you are doing for all of us and our country." He looked surprised and said, "Thank you, ma'am."

When I got to the gate, there he was again, waiting to board the flight I was on. So I walked over, sat beside him for a moment, said that I hoped he was on leave, going home. He told me he had been flying for 25 hours, from Baghdad to Shannon, and now Dallas, with an hour to wait for the flight to his home town. He had a two-week leave at home, so I gave him my card and asked him to e-mail me his APO address when he returned, saying I would send him some things to read. He said he would like that, but it would be three weeks before I would hear from him. Then he put in my hand a rumpled Iraqi bill—5,000 dinars. I said I couldn't take his money and he smiled and said, "Ma'am, I want you to have it; it's not even worth a dollar." I told him I would frame it and put it in my office as a reminder of him and all of our young soldiers.

I thanked him and went back to my seat, thinking of this 18-year-old gunner, working in 125-degree heat in Iraq with no complaints. After a moment, I trotted back and pressed a coin in his hand. General William Ward had given it to me several weeks before when I spoke to the Military Child Education Coalition Conference in Houston, and I said, "I have been carrying this with me for good luck. Now I want you to carry it for good luck." He said, "Oh ma'am, I can't accept this. It's a General's coin." (Military leaders, at times, have special coins that they present in recognition of an individual's contribution.) I said, "I have accepted your Iraqi money, which I will cherish always. You have to accept General Ward's coin. I know he would be honored that I've given it to you."

When we landed, the young soldier's family was waiting: mother, father, grandparents, and two little brothers about five and seven, dressed in the same 1st Infantry uniform he was wearing. I've never seen such hugs. Two little soldiers welcoming their big brother home for two weeks—while one little brother was in his arms, the other was hugging the young soldier's leg.

So the coin is traveling—and it couldn't be in better hands. It was a poignant moment with a tired young soldier, modest, quiet, no complaints, just doing his job, as I hear over and over. And he is carrying my coin for good luck. I'm waiting to hear from him, for I want to stuff a Post Office box with things to read and some amenities that are hard to find in Baghdad and send it to that young gunner far from home.

These are the faces I remember, the faces in the crowd that bring alive a war that can seem far away to civilians. So far, I have never heard one complaint—they always say, "Just doing my job, thank you."

And when I receive e-mail from young 2nd Lieutenants serving in Iraq, graduates of West Point's Class of 2005, there are no complaints, only messages about how great their people are. I find new energy and appreciation when I think of these young faces, where they are, and the spirit within that enables them to serve so selflessly.

When I escape the airport and reach the auditorium, the hotel ballroom, the conference center, I find more faces in the crowd that give me new energy. I've just come from a small luncheon, six of us around a table in New York with Her Royal Highness, the Princess Aisha of Jordan, who is the sister of the King. She is also a brigadier general in the Jordanian Army, a graduate of Dana Hall High School of Wellesley,

Massachusetts, and of Sandhurst, as well. General James Peake, former surgeon general of the U.S. Army, now retired, who is the C.O.O. of Project Hope, brought us together. It was an inspiring hour and a half, for the issues we discussed, women's health and corporate social responsibility, are global issues, as imperative in Pennsylvania as in Jordan—common issues, common language, common ground, as we find so often in the work of our Leader to Leader Institute.

A face in the crowd rarely turns out to be a vibrant, committed young global leader who also is a mother, a royal princess, a brigadier general on active duty, and a parachutist. We share a common bottom line, changing lives and building the healthy community that cares about all of its people.

Faces in the crowd have an amazing way of emerging in their own way, their own right, not just numbers, all of them with names and faces, part of our own world. The most vivid faces in my special crowds are the faces of college and university students here and abroad, and cadets at West Point. There is something about this current generation that is less cynical, more interested in service than some earlier generations. They inspire me. The e-mail messages I receive when I get home are very moving. They relate to "Leadership is a matter of how to be, not how to do," and "to serve is to live" connects in a special way.

This article originally appeared in *Leader to Leader*, Issue 43, Winter 2007.

The Winter of Our Concern

*L*eader to Leader is almost 10 years old and the Drucker Foundation/ Leader to Leader Institute celebrated its 15th anniversary in May. Lots of anniversaries around here.

As I look back to that first issue of the journal in 1996, I remember it was the beginning of a dream, an expectation that great thought leaders might share their ideas, their stories, their inspiration with the leaders we would serve in all three sectors—the nonprofit leaders and their partners in business and government. We had just begun calling the nonprofit sector "the social sector," agreeing that "nonprofit states only what we are not; it is in the social sector where we find the greatest success in meeting social needs."

That was then.

This is the winter of 2006 and we live in a very different world. Even the most prescient of us could not foresee the day in September that would change our world forever. In those days before 9/11, I remember quoting Peter Drucker, who in 2000 said, "The next ten years will be years of great political turmoil in many parts of the world, including the United States." I often followed his observation with the comment, "Peter Drucker is not a pessimist, but he is very sober about the next ten years."

We are now halfway through that decade and the daily headlines, the daily broadcasts, the ubiquitous Internet, all underscore the sad reality of Peter's observation.

The World Trade Center, New Orleans and the Gulf Coast, the tsunami, the wars affecting millions around the world, including the United States, frame this winter of our concern. Hunger, lack of medical care, the state of public education, the growing disparities, the divisive issues of race and class affecting our country have had a massive impact upon society. This doesn't sound much like a happy 10th anniversary message, does it?

Yet in the very magnitude, the complexity, the context of our lives as leaders, leading in tenuous times, there are the most magnificent, most compelling, most significant opportunities to lead, find solutions, and rebuild the healthy community.

For leaders in all three sectors determined to help build the healthy, diverse, inclusive community that cares about all of its people, there is a new appreciation that when we build the healthy community, it is for the greater good. And even for a leader with little concern about the greater good, there is the reality that a sick and ailing community cannot produce the healthy, energetic, productive workforce our enterprises demand if indeed they are to be viable and even present at the end of this turbulent decade.

If the mountain of challenges we face seems formidable, let's look at some of those "rock climbers" who are taking the lead to build a better future.

In September 2005, Chevron for the ninth year brought a wonderfully diverse group of 28 social sector leaders to the Chevron Management Seminar in San Ramon, California. Leaders from six countries participated—Angola, Indonesia, Nigeria, the Philippines, Colombia, and the United States of America.

Marshall Goldsmith and I had opened the first of these seminars in September 1996. In September 2005, we had the privilege of once again as a team partnering with a great corporation as it moved beyond the walls of its own corporate success to provide a powerful leadership-management learning opportunity for 28 social sector leaders—a partnership in changing lives and building community.

Last September, General Erik Shinseki, retired, a former chief of staff of the U.S. Army, and I spoke at the opening of the seminar. This year, Marshall Goldsmith, the top executive consultant (recently profiled in *Forbes* and a founding member of the Drucker Foundation/Leader to Leader Institute Board), and I partnered again to open the Chevron conference.

Continuity, the commitment to bringing superior leadership and management learning to a richly diverse group of social sector leaders every year, is a powerful statement of corporate commitment to strengthening the social sector and building the healthy community. The Chevron Management Seminar was not a one-shot splash, great PR and that's the end. It is a documented long-term investment in community, in leadership development beginning with Texaco, then Chevron-Texaco, now Chevron Management Seminar. Same commitment—same results.

Other rock climbers: a few months ago a small group of university presidents from the United States held their own retreat and chose the University of Oxford as the place to gather for their "Oxford Conclave on Global Ethics and the Changing University Presidency." I was invited to join them as they examined, challenged, and focused not on their own desks, their own leadership imperatives, but on two of the most significant issues of our times. I had the honor of joining these visionaries to speak on leadership and ethics, and then to join the discussion for four days. It was inspiring to see this small group of presidents not content to deal only with the daily challenges of their own university leadership but moving beyond the walls to examine two universal issues.

Of course, rock climbers are found everywhere—not just in organizations. Shortly after Katrina devastated New Orleans, three remarkable college students from Duke University, seeing thousands of people stranded by inadequate rescue efforts, decided to take action. These rock climbers, as reported by South Carolina's *Herald-Sun* newspaper, drove their small Hyundai 12 hours to reach New Orleans, posed as journalists to slip inside the flooded city, and evacuated three women and a man. The next day they went back in and rescued three more people in their small car. Seven people who weren't receiving help from authorities were saved and put on a bus to Texas. Rock climbers see a need and take action. They lead by example.

The people left behind in New Orleans were rock climbers as well, even as the waters surged around them. Reports from two California paramedics who were stranded by the flooding tell of maintenance workers who used a forklift to carry the sick and disabled; of engineers who rigged up and kept the generators running; of nurses who took over for mechanical ventilators and spent many hours manually breathing for unconscious patients; of mechanics who helped hot-wire any car that could be found to carry people to safety; and of food service workers who scoured the commercial kitchens to improvise communal meals for hundreds of those stranded. These are profound examples of the power of human spirit.

I dwell on these stories because I write this message in September just as Hurricane Katrina has devastated New Orleans and the Gulf Coast and the country and the world are responding. When this issue of *Leader to Leader* is published in the winter of 2006, we will have before us lessons learned in the devastation, the human tragedies, the personal and institutional responses, the leadership given and not given, the human response to unbelievable human needs—tragic lessons in leadership, inspiring lessons in leadership.

Hurricane Katrina is a sad note on which to end this winter message to the remarkable people who have been part of our *Leader to Leader* family—rock climbers all. We choose the mountain we climb, and we choose our companions for the climb. It is a privilege to make the journey with you.

This article originally appeared in *Leader to Leader*, Issue 39, Winter 2006.

Circles of Inclusion

I've known for a long time that my work—my style of leadership and management—is inclusive and circular. For me, life is circular.

As I wrote in one of my first columns for this journal ("Managing in a World That Is Round," *Leader to Leader,* Number 2, Fall 1996, available on our Web site at leadertoleader.org), the old, rigid hierarchies, with people in boxes and the matching hierarchical language of top-bottom, up-down, superior-subordinate, are disappearing from the world of effective organizations, agencies, corporations. The new world of flexible, fluid management systems, structures, and practices is reflected in an inclusive, circular organizational culture that reminds us that "culture is the beliefs and values practiced by an organization." Inclusion is a powerful value: when we open up the organization, dispersing the leadership and including people from across the enterprise, there is a new energy, a new synergy. The old boxes communicated separation and could never provide the inclusive mindset and "managing in a world that is round" that moves us to new levels of engagement, inquiry, performance, and results.

Today for leaders in all three sectors the great challenge is leading change—with innovation the daily discipline. Peter Drucker wrote in his seminal article, "The Next Society—Survey of the Near Future," in *The Economist*: "To survive and succeed, every organization will have to turn itself into a change agent. The most effective way to manage change successfully is to create it. But experience has shown that grafting innovation on to a traditional enterprise does not work. The enterprise has to become a change agent. It requires systematic innovation. The point of becoming a change agent is that it changes the mindset of the entire organization."

Today, organizations in all three sectors are becoming change agents, developing powerful initiatives based on an inclusive, circular mindset that opens up the future for themselves, their constituents, those they serve, those they serve with, and the community. Here are a few examples.

Recently I was invited to write an article for the January-February issue of the Points of Light Foundation's magazine, *Volunteer Leadership*. I have a special interest in the remarkable work of the Points of Light Foundation and its Volunteer Centers, always in the vanguard, in measurable and documented results. (I serve on its National Board and was one of five citizens in a Presidential Commission charged by President George Bush, in 1990, to develop a plan for a new foundation to be called the Points of Light Foundation.)

The editor of the journal asked me to look at the challenges facing large national organizations with local councils, centers, affiliates, or units. Speaking to many conferences of large national organizations with local affiliates, I'm observing a renewed interest in seeing the total organization as a Movement, appreciating the Movement as more than local units delivering services to the customers on the ground, and the national organization providing resources, a national voice, advocacy. Serving as chairman of the Volunteers of America and chairman of the Leader to Leader Institute, and having been CEO of Girl Scouts of the USA, I have seen firsthand how the power and influence of a great national or international Movement goes far beyond the efforts of an organization separated by levels, tradition, or us-them mindset. An effective Movement unleashes new energy, results, trust, and cohesion that the old perceived separation of local and national groups could not provide. One great Movement, mobilizing around mission and changing lives, powered by circular engagement, leaves the old hierarchy behind and sends a powerful message.

Central Lutheran Church in downtown Minneapolis provides another example of an inclusive, circular mindset. Central Lutheran Church, along with several other organizations, spearheaded the State of Faith project to determine what business executives were looking for from their churches. The church wanted to form stronger ties to businesses and their employees located in downtown Minneapolis. Interest in the project soared, leading to a national publication and the decision to hold a conference to explore the implications of the research. "The

State of Faith: Ethics in the Workplace" was not just for members of the clergy but equally for business leaders, since the authors of the study and the planners of the conference believed that principled, ethical business leaders are called to do what they do, just as the clergy is called.

The conference organizers knew about my philosophy of The Call, expressed as I spoke to the Dwight D. Eisenhower Institute National Security Conference in Washington, where I said to 200 admirals and generals and civilian leaders responsible for our country's national security, "You are called to do what you do—every person in this room is called to do what you do. For you, it is never a job—you are called."

When invited to speak to more than 300 men and women, clergy, business, and community leaders in Minnesota last September, the subject they gave me was, "We Are Called." It was a powerful conference with rich collaboration across all three sectors, with remarkable results, and it will be repeated with even greater inclusion.

Another example comes from China, when I was there two years ago, with a Drucker Foundation Team, providing seven days of Leadership and Management in the 21st Century Seminars to leaders in all three sectors. We reached 2,000 business, government, and nonprofit leaders in that week in Beijing, Shenzhen, and Dongguan. In the seminars, I used two charts—both circular—one "Managing in a World That Is Round" and the other "Journey to Transformation." They looked particularly handsome on the ceiling-to-floor blue silk panels that our Bright China Management Institute partners designed.

Our final seminar went from eight o'clock in the morning to noon, when we left for the airport and the long flight home. We never had a more responsive audience. As the governor of Dongguan was thanking our team for that closing seminar in a week filled with wonderful engagement and appreciation, he turned to me and pointing to the two circles said, "Thank you for bringing to China the culture of roundness. The circle was a value of ancient China; it is a value of China, today. Thank you."

In that touching moment, saying good-bye to a wonderfully responsive audience of 800 leaders—business, government, party, the emerging nonprofit leaders, and university students, I remembered a time long ago, in a small town in western Pennsylvania, when I discovered the value of the circle, of circular management, in my first Girl Scouts Council job. I carried this discovery with me, six years later, when I was called to New York to work for the Girl Scouts at a national and international level. The circle was a value at the local level; it was a value at the national and global level on a journey to transformation.

A final example of the mind-set that transcends the old hierarchy comes from our work with the U.S. Army. In *Leader to Leader* and our newsletters, in our own conferences and speeches, we've often mentioned with great appreciation "Army Leadership: Be, Know, Do" (the U.S. Army's 1999 leadership manual), and hundreds of civilians have inquired about access to that manual. Fortunately, it is unclassified and here is the good news: in February, a long and mutually appreciative circular partnership of The Conference Board, the U.S. Army, Leader to Leader Institute (formerly the Drucker Foundation), and Jossey-Bass/John Wiley & Sons will publish a new leadership resource based on the Army manual for leaders in all three sectors, for leaders everywhere: *Be, Know, Do—Leadership the Army Way.* This will be the 18th book the Drucker Foundation/Leader to Leader Institute has published, once again with partners, and once again a book that will move across all three sectors, as helpful to the leaders in business and government as to social sector leaders. It will travel around the world, as have our other 17 books (now also in 17 languages) for the message of *Be, Know, Do* is global and circular.

We could fill this journal with examples of the power of the circle, the culture of roundness. All our experience in all three sectors, in our own country or with colleagues around the globe, confirms that when we move into a position, a relationship, a structure, or an organization, it is the circles, the inclusive circles, that free up the spirit, the ingenuity, the creative spirits of our people and ourselves—the spirit within the leader that transcends and transforms.

This article originally appeared in *Leader to Leader,* Issue 32, Spring 2004.

INDEX